Though flowers fall
I have never forgotten you

꽃이 져도 나는 너를 잊은 적 없다

Though flowers fall I have never forgotten you

Original poems copyright © 2016 by Jeong Ho-seung
English translations copyright © 2016 by Brother Anthony of Taizé and Susan Hwang

All Rights Reserved.
No part of this book may be reproduced or utilized in any form or by any means without the written permission of the publisher.

Published in 2025 by Seoul Selection
B1, 6 Samcheong-ro, Jongno-gu, Seoul 03062, Korea

Phone: (82-2) 734-9567
Fax: (82-2) 734-9563
Email: hankinseoul@gmail.com
Website: www.seoulselection.com

ISBN: 979-11-89809-88-1 03810
Printed in the Republic of Korea

* *Though flowers fall I have never forgotten you* is translated and published with the support of the Literature Translation Institute of Korea (LTI Korea).

The Collected Poems of **Jeong Ho-seung** 　　　　정호승 시선집

Though flowers fall
I have never forgotten you

꽃이 져도 나는 너를 잊은 적 없다

Translated by **Brother Anthony of Taizé** and **Susan Hwang**

Seoul Selection

Contents

A Word from the Poet 시인의 말 11

Part1

To Daffodils 수선화에게 15
Flower-Falling Evening 꽃 지는 저녁 17
The South Han River 남한강 19
Hanging a Wind Chime 풍경 달다 21
About a Beach 바닷가에 대하여 23
Snail 달팽이 25
Ants 개미 27
The Well 우물 29
For Chopped Octopus 산낙지를 위하여 31
Sehando*: Winter Landscape 세한도 33
Sudeoksa Temple Station 수덕사역 35
Insu Peak 인수봉 37
No Memories 추억이 없다 39
A Train 기차 41
Spring Snow 봄눈 43
Responsibility of a Kiss 키스에 대한 책임 45
Love 사랑 47
For a Reed 갈대를 위하여 49
A Rouge-Stained Cigarette Butt is Sexy 루즈가 묻은 담배꽁초는 섹시하다 51

Tattered Stars 누더기별 53
Ignorance 모른다 55

Part 2

Spring Rain 봄비 59
Adoption 입양 61
The River 강물 63
Dear My Love 애인이여 65
To a Leaf 잎새에게 67
The Heart's Desert 마음의 사막 69
Dawn Prayer 새벽 기도 71
I Will Give You All 모두 드리리 73
To You 당신에게 75
Reasons 까닭 77
The Heart inside My Heart 내 마음속의 마음이 79
Waiting 기다림 81
Sleeping Curled like a Prawn 새우잠 83
To the Bitter End 끝끝 내 85
About My First Kiss 첫키스에 대하여 87
Miracles 기적 89
In the Street 거리에서 91
Life-Sized Buddha 등신불 93
I'm Hungry 배가 고프다 95
I Weep Prostrate Before an Orchid 난(蘭) 앞에 엎드려 울다 99
A Single Log Bridge 외나무다리 101
Manggyeongsa Temple 망경사(望鏡寺) 103

Part 3

Icebound 결빙 107

Air 허공 109

Earning my Keep 밥값 111

Resurrection 부활 113

Mother's Milk 모유 115

Angels 천사 117

Crossing 고비 119

Passing a Ginseng Field 인삼밭을 지나며 121

Flower in Water 물의 꽃 123

Bullfight 투우 125

Snow-Damaged Trees 설해목(雪害木) 127

A Mirror 거울 129

Standing before a Notice Board 어느 벽보판 앞에서 131

Flowers 꽃 133

Stars Don't Cry 별들은 울지 않는다 135

Bird Shit 새똥 137

The Water's Shoes 물의 신발 139

Burdens 짐 141

Enough Unhappiness 충분한 불행 143

On Looking at Coffee Spilled on the Floor 바닥에 쏟은 커피를 바라보며 145

I'm Sorry 죄송합니다 147

Prejudice Regarding the Left 왼쪽에 대한 편견 149

The Sea's Saints 바다의 성자 151

Part 4

Living like a Ruined Temple 폐사지처럼 산다 155

Runaway 도망자 157

A Paper Elephant 종이코끼리 159

Sad, Having No Enemy to Love 사랑할 원수가 없어서 슬프다 161

Huibang Falls 희방폭포 163

Silk Road 실크로드 165

In Seoguipo 서귀포에서 167

In Gampo 감포에서 169

The Day Snow First Falls 첫눈 오는 날 171

Blades 칼날 173

Reeds Do Not Weep at Dawn 갈대는 새벽에 울지 않는다 175

Grief to the World, the Savior Has Come. 슬프다 구주 오셨네 177

Spider Lilies at Seonunsa Temple 선운사 상사화 179

Sudeok Inn 수덕여관 181

A Smile 웃음 183

Visit to Simujang* 심우장에 가다 185

Rice Soup 국밥 187

The Other 타인 189

Seen from the Back 뒷모습 191

A White Heron 백로 193

Part 5   195

Bricks 벽돌 197
Stepping Stones 징검다리 199
Chair of Forgiveness 용서의 의자 201
For the Sake of Vanishing Things 사라지는 것들을 위하여 203
Identification Photo 증명사진 205
Water's Flowers 물의 꽃 207
A Spider 거미 209
Epitaph for Birds 새들을 위한 묘비명 211
My Guest Book 나의 방명록 213
A Night's Plastic Greenhouse 밤의 비닐하우스 215
Lee Jung-seop's Room* 이중섭의 방 217
Dasan's Tavern 다산 주막 219
Poetry Books 시집 221
A Snowy Path 눈길 223
Confessing to a Young Zelkova 젊은 느티나무에게 고백함 225
One Night Reading a Braille Poetry Book 점자시집을 읽는 밤 227
At Gwanghwamun Gate 광화문에서 229
Snowstorm 폭설 231
Bupyeong Station 부평역 233
Magnolia 목련 235
The Holy Grail 성배 237
Swamp 늪 239

Translators' Note 번역자의 말 241

시인의 말

시는 고통의 꽃이다. 고통이 없었다면 나는 시를 쓸 수 없었다. 내 인생의 고통은 나로 하여금 시를 쓰게 해주는 은총이자 축복이다. 그동안 내 삶의 고통을 원망하고 분노해왔으나 이제야 조금씩 감사의 마음을 지닐 수 있게 되었다.

수련이 뿌리를 내리고 있는 곳은 인간이 버린 온갖 쓰레기들이 흘러들어와 오염된 흙탕물 속이다. 그곳은 수련의 삶이 이루어지는 현실적 장소로써, 수련은 참으로 고통스러울 것이다. 그러나 고통의 진흙물 속에서도 수련이 피워 올리는 꽃만은 맑고 아름답다. 나는 늘 내 시가 그런 수련과 같아야 한다고 생각해왔다.

수련은 고통 가운데서도 그 더러운 흙탕물을 미워하거나 증오하지는 않았을 것이다. 만일 미움과 증오가 가득 찼다면 그토록 아름다운 꽃을 피워 올릴 수 없었을 것이다. 수련은 흙탕물을 용서하고 받아들이고 참고 견디며 사랑함으로써 아름다운 꽃을 피워 올린 것이다. 시 또한 마찬가지다. 수련이 고통과 용서를 통해 피어난 사랑의 꽃이듯, 시는 결국 사랑을 통해 완성된다.

길을 가다가 다시 수련을 바라본다. 수련은 오직 피어 있을 뿐 아무 말이 없다. 누구를 통해 어떤 과정을 거쳐 어떻게 피어났다고 말하지 않는다. 수련은 침묵함으로써 더욱 아름다울 뿐이다. 꽃의 침묵처럼 시 또한 침묵으로 이루어진다.

시는 침묵의 말이다. 침묵을 배경으로 하지 않으면 시는 이루어지지 않는다. 이 시선집은 내 삶의 고통에 관한 침묵의 말이다.

나는 문학을 믿고 시를 믿는다. 시가 나와 이웃을 구원하고 모든 인간의 고통을 기쁨으로 성화(聖化)시켜 줄 것이라고 믿는다. 아무것도 믿지 않으면 신도 등을 돌린다고 하지 않는가. 시는 내 믿음의 근원이다. 시는 인간을 이해하게 하고 인간을 위로해준다.

2016년 가을

정호승

A Word from the Poet

A poem is the flower of pain. If there had been no pain in my life, I could not have written poetry. My life's pain has been the grace and blessing which enabled me to write poetry. Until now, I have felt resentment and anger toward life's pain, but I have slowly begun to feel grateful for it.

A water lily puts down its roots amid the muddy slime polluted by all kinds of trash that people have thrown away. Thus, the water lily originates in a very real place, and is bound to suffer pain in consequence. Yet the flowers which the water lily produces from that slime of pain are pure and beautiful. I have long reckoned that my poems should resemble the water lily.

Even in the midst of pain, the water lily seems to feel neither dislike nor loathing toward that filthy slime. If it were full of hatred and anger, it would surely not be able to produce such beautiful flowers. The water lily produces beautiful flowers by forgiving the slime and accepting it, patiently enduring it and loving it. Poetry is the same. Just as a water lily is the flower of love that blossoms through pain and forgiveness, a poem is ultimately made perfect through love.

Continuing my journey, I encounter another water lily. The water lily only blooms; it says nothing. It does not explain who made it blossom or how, by what process, it bloomed. The water lily is simply made more beautiful by its silence. Like the flower's silence, a poem, too, is produced through silence.

Poetry is the speech of silence. Without silence as its background, poetry will not arise. This collection of my poems is the speech of silence about my life's pain.

I believe in literature, I believe in poetry. I believe that poetry is something which can save me and my neighbors, can sanctify and transform all human pain into joy. After all, don't some people say that if nobody believes, then God will also turn his back on us? Poetry is the source of my faith. Poetry enables me to understand people, and it comforts people.

Jeong Ho-seung
Autumn, 2016

Part 1

수선화에게

울지 마라
외로우니까 사람이다
살아간다는 것은 외로움을 견디는 일이다
공연히 오지 않는 전화를 기다리지 마라
눈이 오면 눈길을 걸어가고
비가 오면 빗길을 걸어가라
갈대숲에서 가슴검은도요새도 너를 보고 있다
가끔은 하느님도 외로워서 눈물을 흘리신다
새들이 나뭇가지에 앉아 있는 것도 외로움 때문이고
네가 물가에 앉아 있는 것도 외로움 때문이다
산그림자도 외로워서 하루에 한 번씩 마을로 내려온다
종소리도 외로워서 울려퍼진다

To Daffodils

Don't cry.
To be lonely is to be human.
To go on living is to endure loneliness.
Do not wait in vain for the phone call that never comes.
When snow falls, walk on snowy paths,
when rain falls, walk on rainy paths.
A black-breasted longbill is watching you from the bed of reeds.
Sometimes even God is so lonely he weeps.
Birds perch on branches because they are lonely,
and you are sitting beside the stream because you are lonely.
The hill's shadow comes down to the village once a day because it,
    too, is lonely.
And a bell's chime resounds because it, too, is lonely.

꽃 지는 저녁

꽃이 진다고 아예 다 지나
꽃이 진다고 전화도 없나
꽃이 져도 나는 너를 잊은 적 없다
지는 꽃의 마음을 아는 이가
꽃이 진다고 저만 외롭나
꽃이 져도 나는 너를 잊은 적 없다
꽃 지는 저녁에는 배도 고파라

Flower-Falling Evening

Flowers fall, but surely not all flowers fall.
Flowers fall, but surely there are still phones.
Though flowers fall, I have never forgotten you.
He who understands a falling flower
    surely must know he is not the only lonesome one, though
        flowers fall.
Though flowers fall I have never forgotten you.
On evenings when flowers fall, I am still hungry.

남한강

얼어붙은 남한강 한가운데에
나룻배 한 척 떠 있습니다
첫얼음이 얼기 전에 어디론가
멀리 가고파서
제딴에는 먼바다를 생각하다가
그만 얼어붙어버리고 말았습니다
나룻배를 사모하는 남한강 갈대들이
하룻밤 사이에 겨울을 불러들여
아무데도 못 가게 붙들어둔 줄을
나룻배는 저 혼자만 모르고 있습니다

The South Han River

In the middle of the frozen South Han River
floats a ferryboat.
Longing to go somewhere far away
before the first frosts fell
it bethought itself of the distant sea
then ended up frozen in the ice.
That the South Han River reeds that love the ferryboat,
summoned winter in the span of one night
to keep it from going anywhere,
the boat alone does not know.

풍경 달다

운주사 와불님을 뵙고
돌아오는 길에
그대 가슴의 처마끝에
풍경을 달고 돌아왔다
먼데서 바람 불어와
풍경 소리 들리면
보고 싶은 내 마음이
찾아간 줄 알아라

Hanging a Wind Chime

On my way home
after meeting with the reclining Buddha at Unjusa Temple
I hung a wind chime
on the eaves of your heart.
When the wind blows from far away
and the wind chime rings,
know that it is my heart, longing to see you,
that has come to visit.

바닷가에 대하여

누구나 바닷가 하나씩은 자기만의 바닷가가 있는 게 좋다
누구나 바닷가 하나씩은 언제나 찾아갈 수 있는
자기만의 바닷가가 있는 게 좋다
잠자는 지구의 고요한 숨소리를 듣고 싶을 때
지구 위를 걸어가는 새들의 작은 발소리를 듣고 싶을 때
새들과 함께 수평선 위로 걸어가고 싶을 때
친구를 위해 내 목숨을 버리지 못했을 때
서럽게 우는 어머니를 껴안고 함께 울었을 때
모내기가 끝난 무논의 저수지 둑 위에서
자살한 어머니의 고무신 한 짝을 발견했을 때
바다에 뜬 보름달을 향해 촛불을 켜놓고 하염없이
두 손 모아 절을 하고 싶을 때
바닷가 기슭으로만 기슭으로만 끝없이 달려가고 싶을 때
누구나 자기만의 바닷가가 하나씩 있으면 좋다
자기만의 바닷가로 달려가 쓰러지는 게 좋다

About a Beach

For anyone it's good to have one beach as their very own.
For anyone it's good to have one beach as their very own,
one they can visit at any time:
when they want to hear the quiet breathing of the earth in slumber,
when they want to hear the murmuring footsteps of birds walking
    on the earth,
when they want to walk with the birds above the horizon,
when they could not give up their life for a friend,
when they embraced a mournfully weeping mother and wept
    with her,
when they discovered on the bank of a planted rice-field's reservoir
one rubber shoe of a mother who killed herself,
when they want to light candles, then, with hands joined,
bow endlessly to the full moon above the sea,
when they want to keep on running endlessly to the shore, only to
    the shore,
it's good to have one beach as their very own.
It's good to run to one's own beach and collapse.

달팽이

내 마음은 연약하나 껍질은 단단하다
내 껍질은 연약하나 마음은 단단하다
사람들이 외롭지 않으면 길을 떠나지 않듯이
달팽이도 외롭지 않으면 길을 떠나지 않는다

이제 막 기울기 시작한 달은 차돌같이 차다
나의 길은 어느새 풀잎에 젖어 있다
손에 주전자를 들고 아침이슬을 밟으며
내가 가야 할 길 앞에서 누가 오고 있다

죄 없는 소년이다
소년이 무심코 나를 밟고 간다
아마 아침이슬인 줄 알았나 보다

Snail

My heart is soft, but my shell is hard.
My shell is soft, but my heart is hard.
Just as people never set out unless they are lonely,
a snail also never sets out unless it is lonely.

The moon that has just begun to set is as cold as stone.
Before I know it my path is wet with blades of grass.
Carrying a kettle and treading on morning dew
somebody is coming down the path I must advance along.

It is an innocent boy.
The boy treads heedlessly over me as he passes by.
I suppose he mistook me for morning dew.

개미

달빛 아래 개미들이 기어간다
한평생 잠들지 못한 개미란 개미는 다 강가로 나가
일제히 칼을 간다
저마다 마음의 빈자리에 고이 간직한 칼을 꺼내어
조금도 쉬지 않고 간다
달빛은 푸르다
강물 소리는 들리지 않는다
개미들이 일제히 칼끝을 치켜세우고
자기의 목을 찌른다

Ants

Ants are crawling under the moonlight.
Any and all ants that remain sleepless for a lifetime all head for the river bank,
and all sharpen their swords.
Each quietly draws a precious sword from an empty spot in its heart
and sharpens it without a moment's rest.
The moonlight shines blue.
There is no sound of the river flowing.
Together, the ants all raise their swords
and pierce their throats.

우물

길을 가다가 우물을 들여다보았다
누가 낮달을 초승달로 던져놓았다
길을 가다가 다시 우물을 들여다보았다
쑥떡이 든 보따리를 머리에 이고
홀로 기차를 타시는 어머니가 보였다
다시 길을 떠났다가 돌아와 우물을 들여다보았다
평화시장의 흐린 형광등 불빛 아래
미싱을 돌리다 말고
물끄러미 네가 나를 쳐다보고 있었다
나는 너를 만나러 우물에 뛰어들었다
어머니가 보따리를 풀어
쑥떡 몇 개를 건네주셨다
너는 보이지 않고 어디선가
미싱 돌아가는 소리만 들렸다

The Well

While walking along, I looked into a well.
Someone had thrown in the daytime moon as a crescent.
Walking further along, I again looked into the well.
I saw my mother boarding a train alone
with a bundle of mugwort rice-cake on her head.
After setting off again, I turned back and again looked into the well.
Instead of turning a sewing machine wheel
under the faint fluorescent lights of Peace Market
you were staring up at me.
I jumped into the well to meet you.
Mother undid her bundle
and handed me a few pieces of mugwort rice-cake.
There was no sign of you, only the sound of
a sewing machine still running somewhere.

산낙지를 위하여

신촌 뒷골목에서 술을 먹더라도
이제는 참기름에 무친 산낙지는 먹지 말자
낡은 플라스틱 접시 위에서
산낙지의 잘려진 발들이 꿈틀대는 동안
바다는 얼마나 서러웠겠니
우리가 산낙지의 다리 하나를 입에 넣어
우물우물거리며 씹어먹는 동안
바다는 또 얼마나 많은
절벽 아래로 뛰어내렸겠니
산낙지의 죽음에도 품위가 필요하다
산낙지는 죽어가면서도 바다를 그리워한다
온몸이 토막토막난 채로
산낙지가 있는 힘을 다해 꿈틀대는 것은
마지막으로 한 번만 더
바다의 어머니를 보려는 것이다

For Chopped Octopus

From now on, even when drinking in Sinchon's back alleys
let's not eat chopped octopus dipped in sesame oil.
While the tentacles sliced from an octopus squirmed
on an old plastic plate,
just how sad the sea must have felt;
while we put one octopus leg in our mouth
and smacked our lips while chewing it,
just how many cliffs
the sea must have hurled itself down from;
even an octopus's death demands dignity.
Even as it dies, an octopus longs for the sea.
An octopus goes on squirming with all its might
even after its body has been chopped to pieces
because it wants one last time
to see its mother in the sea.

세한도

영등포역 어느 뒷골목에서 봤다고 하고
청량리역 어느 무료급식소에서 봤다고 하는
아버지를 찾아 한겨울 내내
서울을 떠돌다가
동부시립병원 행려병동으로 실려가
하루에도 몇 명씩 죽어나가는 행려병자들을 보고 돌아와
늙은 소나무 한 그루 청정히 눈을 맞고 서 있는
아버지의 텅 빈 방문 앞에 무릎을 꿇고 앉다
바람은 차고 달은 춥다
솔가지에 내린 눈은 더 이상 아무 데도 내릴 데가 없다
젊은 날 모내기를 끝내고 찍은
아버지의 빛바랜 사진 옆에 걸려 있는
세한도 속으로
새 한 마리 날아와 앉아 춥다

Sehando*: Winter Landscape

I went wandering through Seoul
all winter long looking for Father, whom
some said they had seen in a back-alley near Yeongdeungpo station,
while others said a soup kitchen near Cheongnyangni Station;
then I was taken to the vagrants' ward of East Seoul City Hospital,
only to see numerous sick vagrants die there each day before
   going home,
and now I kneel before Father's empty room
where one old pine tree stands pure under falling snow.
The wind is icy, the moon feels cold.
The snow that had fallen on the pine tree's branches left no room for
   any more snow to fall.
Beside the faded photo of Father
taken in his youth after planting the rice hangs Sehando
into which one bird flies and perches, cold.

---

* Sehando (winter landscape) is a famous ink-painting by Chusa Kim Jeong-hui (1786 – 1856) showing a simple hut dominated by a few straggling pines.

수덕사역

꽃을 버리고 기차를 타다
꽃을 버리고 수덕사역에 내리다

수덕사로 달팽이 한 마리 기어가다
수덕사로 개미 한 마리 기어가다

해는 저물고
수덕사로 가는 눈길
발은 없고 발자국만 남아 있다

악!

Sudeoksa Temple Station

I throw away flowers and board the train.
I throw away flowers and alight at Sudeoksa Temple station.

A snail crawls toward Sudeoksa Temple.
An ant crawls toward Sudeoksa Temple.

The sun sets.
On the snowy road to Sudeoksa Temple
there are no feet, only footprints remain.

Ouch!

인수봉

바라보지 않아도 바라보고
기다리지 않아도 기다리고
올라가지 않아도 올라가

만나지 않아도 만나고
내려가지 않아도 내려가고
무너지지 않아도 무너져

슬프지 아니하랴
슬프지 아니하랴

사람들은 사랑할 때
사랑을 모른다
사랑이 다 끝난 뒤에서야 문득
인수봉을 바라본다

Insu Peak

To look up even when the other does not.
To wait even when the other does not.
To climb up even when the other does not.

To meet even when the other does not.
To climb down even when the other does not.
To crumble even when the other does not.

Can one be anything but sorrowful?
Can one be anything but sorrowful?

When people are in love
they know nothing of love;
it's only when love is all over that, suddenly
they look up at Insu Peak.

추억이 없다

나무에게는 무덤이 없다
바람에게는 무덤이 없다
깨꽃이 지고 메밀꽃이 져도
꽃들에게는 무덤이 없다

나에게는 추억이 없다
추억으로 걸어가던 들판이 없다
첫눈 오는 날 첫키스를 나누던
그 집 앞 골목길도 사라지고 없다

추억이 없으면 무덤도 없다
추억이 없으면 사랑도 없다
꽃샘바람 부는 이 봄날에
꽃으로 피어나던 사람도 없다

No Memories

Trees have no tombs.
Winds have no tombs.
The salvia flowers wither, the buckwheat flowers fade
yet flowers have no tombs.

I have no memories.
The fields I'd walked in, memories are not there.
Even the alley in front of that house
where I shared my first kiss as the first snow fell has vanished
    and gone.

If you have no memories you have no grave.
If you have no memories you have no love.
On this spring day as a chill wind blows
I have nobody who once blossomed into a flower.

기차

역마다 불이 꺼졌다
떠나간 기차를 용서하라
기차도 때로는 침묵이 필요하다
굳이 수색쯤 어디 아니더라도
그 어느 영원한 선로 밖에서
서로 포기하지 않으면
사랑할 수 없다

A Train

The lights are out in every station.
Forgive the departed trains.
Even trains need silence now and then.
It may not be around somewhere like Susaek
but unless we give each other up
away from such everlasting tracks
love is not possible.

봄눈

봄눈이 내리면
그대 결코
다른 사람에게 눈물을 보이지 말라
봄눈이 내리면
그대 결코
절벽 위를 무릎으로 걸어가지 말라
봄눈이 내리는 날
내 그대의 따뜻한 집이 되리니
그대 가슴의 무덤을 열고
봄눈으로 만든 눈사람이 되리니
우리들에게 가장 필요한 것은
사랑과 용서였다고
올해도 봄눈으로 내리는
나의 사람아

Spring Snow

If spring snow should fall
you must never
let anyone see your tears.
If spring snow should fall
you must never
walk on your knees along a cliff.
On days when spring snow falls
I will become your warm home;
opening the tomb of your breast
I will become a snowman made of spring snow;
what we need most
is love and forgiveness,
so you said,
falling this year again as spring snow.

키스에 대한 책임

키스를 하고 돌아서자 밤이 깊었다
지구 위의 모든 입술들은 잠이 들었다
적막한 나의 키스는 이제 어디로 가야 할 것인가
너의 눈물과 죽음을 책임질 수 있을 것인가
빌딩과 빌딩 사이로 낡은 초승달이 떠 있는 골목길
밤은 초승달을 책임지고 있다
초승달은 새벽을 책임지고 있다

Responsibility of a Kiss

When I turned around after a kiss, the night had deepened.
All the lips on earth have fallen asleep.
Where should my lonely kiss go now, then?
Would it be able to take responsibility for your tears, your death?
In this alley where a shabby new moon has risen
between one building and another
the night is taking responsibility for the new moon.
The new moon is taking responsibility for daybreak.

사랑

강가에 초승달 뜬다
연어떼 돌아오는 소리가 들린다
나그네 한 사람이 술에 취해
강가에 엎드려 있다
연어 한 마리가 나그네의 가슴에
뜨겁게 산란을 하고
고요히 숨을 거둔다

Love

Beside the river, the new moon is rising.
There is a sound of salmon shoals returning.
One traveler, drunk,
is lying prostrate beside the river.
One salmon warmly spawns
in the traveler's breast,
then silently breathes its last.

갈대를 위하여

눈보라가 친다 사라지지 마라
눈보라가 친다 흩어지지 마라
눈보라가 친다 길이 끊어진다
이미 살아갈 날들까지 길은 다 끊어진다

눈을 떠라 눈을 떠라 눈보라 사이로
언뜻언뜻 넋들을 내비치지 마라
가지 마라 가지 마라 눈보라 사이로
혼절한 발자국들을 남기지 마라

사랑이 깊으면 증오도 깊다
눈보라 사이로 밤열차는 지나간다
피리소리는 끊어지고 바람소리만 들린다
쓰러지지 않아야만 뿌리는 뿌리다
흙을 움켜잡고 있을 때만 뿌리는 뿌리다

For a Reed

Snow is blowing hard. Do not disappear.
Snow is blowing hard. Do not run away.
Snow is blowing hard. The road is cut off.
Even to the days still to be lived the roads are all cut off.

Open your eyes, open your eyes amidst the snowstorm,
do not let flashes of your soul be seen.
Don't go, don't go amidst the snowstorm,
do not leave behind faint footprints.

When love is deep, hate is also deep.
The night train passes through the snowstorm.
The sound of flutes has ceased, only the sound of wind is heard.
Only if you do not collapse will your roots be roots.
Only when you grasp the earth firmly will your roots be roots.

루즈가 묻은 담배꽁초는 섹시하다

새벽 미사가 끝나자 눈이 내린다
어깨를 구부리고 눈을 맞으며 집으로 돌아가는 골목길
롱부츠를 신은 여자가 가로등 불빛 아래 담배를 피우며 서 있다
누구를 기다리는 것일까
마지막으로 아들의 얼굴이라도 한번 더 보기 위하여 찾아온 것일까
큰수녀님은 싸리빗자루로 성당 앞에 내리는 눈을 쓸고
나는 십자가에 매달려 있다가 기어내려온 사내처럼
알몸의 마음으로 조심스럽게 여자 앞을 지나간다
여자는 눈송이 사이로 길게 연기를 내뿜으며
입술을 내던지듯 담배꽁초를 휙 내던진다
눈길에 떨어진
붉은 루즈가 묻은 담배꽁초는 섹시하다
만나기 전에 이미 헤어지고
헤어지기 전에 이미 만난 적이 있었던가
눈은 내리는데
가로등 불빛 아래 하루살이떼처럼 눈송이는 날리는데
여자는 다시 담배에 불을 붙인다

A Rouge-Stained Cigarette Butt is Sexy

By the time early morning Mass is over, snow is falling.
In the alleys on my way home, shoulders hunched under the snow,
a woman wearing tall boots is standing under a street lamp smoking
    a cigarette.
Who is she waiting for?
Has she come hoping for one last glimpse of her son's face?
The sister-in-charge is sweeping away the snow falling in front of
    the church
while I, feeling like the fellow who came crawling down after
    hanging on the cross,
pass cautiously with a naked heart in front of the woman.
Exhaling a long stream of smoke amid the snowflakes
she tosses away the cigarette butt as if tossing away her lips.
Dropped on the snowy road,
the cigarette butt stained with crimson rouge is sexy.
Had they already parted before meeting, and
had they already met before parting?
Snow is falling,
snowflakes are whirling under the street lamp like a swarm of
    mayflies,
the woman lights another cigarette.

누더기별

사람이 다니는 눈길 위로
누더기가 된 낙엽들이 걸어간다
낙엽이 다니는 눈길 위로
누더기가 된 사람들이 걸어간다
그 뒤를 쓸쓸히 개미 한 마리 따른다
그 뒤를 쓸쓸히 내가 따른다
누더기가 되고 나서 내 인생이 편안해졌다
누더기가 되고 나서 비로소 별이 보인다
개미들도 누더기별이 되는 데에는
평생이 걸린다

Tattered Stars

On the snowy road people take
fallen leaves turned to tatters are walking.
On the snowy road taken by leaves
people turned to tatters are walking.
One ant is following forlornly behind them.
Behind it I am following forlornly.
Once I had turned to tatters my life grew peaceful.
Only after turning to tatters can the stars finally be seen.
For ants, too, it takes a whole lifetime
to turn into tattered stars.

모른다

사람들은 사랑이 끝난 뒤에도 사랑을 모른다
사랑이 다 끝난 뒤에도 끝난 줄을 모른다
창 밖에 내리던 누더기눈도
내리다 지치면 숨을 죽이고
새들도 지치면 돌아갈 줄 아는데
사람들은 누더기가 되어서도 돌아갈 줄 모른다

Ignorance

People know nothing of love, even when love is over.
Even when love is all over, they do not know it.
Even the flurries of snow falling outside the window,
when weary after falling, know how to hold their breath,
and birds, when weary, know how to turn back
but people, even when they're tattered, do not know how to
   turn back.

Part 2

봄비

어느날
썩은 내 가슴을
조금 파보았다
흙이 조금 남아 있었다
그 흙에
꽃씨를 심었다

어느날
꽃씨를 심은 내 가슴이
너무 궁금해서
조금 파보려고 하다가
봄비가 와서
그만두었다

Spring Rain

One day
I dug
into my rotten breast.
There was still some soil left.
I sowed flower seeds
in that soil.

One day,
very curious
about my breast, where I had sown flower seeds,
I began to dig into it.
Then spring rain fell
so I stopped.

입양

누가 나를 입양하겠다고 한다
아무짝에도 쓸모없는
이미 헌옷박스에 버려진 나를
하늘의 호적에 올리고
데려가겠다고 한다
이왕이면 비행기를 타고 갔으면 좋겠다
이번에 나를 입양할 부모는
토성 근처 어느 별에 사는
별지기라고 한다

Adoption

Someone is proposing to adopt me.
Good for nothing,
I had already been thrown into a box for old clothes.
But they want to add my name to heaven's family register
and take me with them.
In that case I hope we travel by plane.
It seems the parents adopting me this time
are starkeepers
on some star near Saturn.

강물

그대로 두어라 흐르는 것이 물이다
사랑의 용서도 용서함도 구하지 말고
청춘도 청춘의 돌무덤도 돌아보지 말고
그대로 두어라 흐르는 것이 길이다
흐느끼는 푸른 댓잎 하나
날카로운 붉은 난초잎 하나
강의 중심을 향해 흘러가면 그뿐
그동안 강물을 가로막고 있었던 것은
내가 아니었다 절망이었다
그동안 나를 가로막고 있었던 것은
강물이 아니었다 희망이었다

The River

Just let it be. What flows on is water.
Do not seek love's forgiveness or any forgiving,
do not look back on youth or youth's stone tomb,
Let it be. What flows on is the way.
If one sobbing green bamboo leaf,
one pointed crimson orchid leaf,
go flowing toward the center of the river, that's all.
It was not I who had constantly been blocking
the river. It was desperation.
It was not the river that had been blocking
me all the while. It was hope.

애인이여

잠들지 말고 기차를 타라
기차가 달려가 멈춘 그 강가
갈대숲에 버려진 은장도를 주워
정처 없는 내 가슴에 내리꽂아다오
피에 젖어 바다가 흐느낄 때까지
흐느끼다 수평선이 사라질 때까지
은장도를 꽂은 채 내 싸늘한
사체 한 토막 바닷가에 던져다오
파도에 어리는 희디흰 달빛으로
달빛을 물고 나는 기러기떼로
나 죽어 살리니 애인이여
밤이 오면 잠들지 말고 기차를 타라

Dear My Love

Do not sleep, catch a train.
At the riverside where the train will go speeding, then stop
pick up the silver knife discarded in the reedbed
and plunge it into my feckless heart,
until the seashore sobs, soaked in blood,
until the horizon sobs then vanishes.
Cast one piece of my cold corpse,
transfixed with the knife, onto the shore.
By the pure white moonlight glistening on the waves,
by the flocks of geese that fly biting the moonlight,
I die, vanish, so dear my love,
when evening comes,
do not sleep, but catch a train.

잎새에게

하느님도 쓸쓸하시다
하느님도 인간에게 사랑을 바라다가 쓸쓸하시다
오늘의 마지막 열차가 소리없이 지나가는 들녘에 서서
사랑은 죽음보다 강한지 알 수 없어라
그대는 광한루 돌담길을 홀로 걷다가
많은 것을 잃었으나 모든 것을 잃지는 않았나니
미소로서 그대를 통과하던 밝은 햇살과
온몸을 간지럽히던 싸락눈의 정다움을 기억하시라
우듬지 위로 날마다 감옥을 만들고
감옥이 너무 너르다고 생각한 것은 잘못이었나니
그대 가슴 위로 똥을 누고 가는 저 새들이
그 얼마나 아름다우냐
사랑하고 싶은 인간이 없어
하느님도 쓸쓸한 저녁 무렵
삶은 때때로 키스처럼 반짝거린다

To a Leaf

God is lonely, too.
God, too, is lonely after hoping for love from people.
Standing out in the fields as the day's last train passes soundlessly
there is no way of knowing if love is stronger than death.
After walking alone along the stone-walled path round Gwanghallu
you lost many things but did not lose everything
so you should recall the sunlight that passed through you with
   a smile
and the affection of the hail that once tickled you all over.
You should forgive last night's storm that shook you to the very roots
and the arrogance of the soldier ants running wild with swords
   drawn.
It was an error to build a prison in the treetops every day
then think that the prison was too spacious,
yet how beautiful are the birds
that fly above your breast releasing droppings.
At evenings when God too is lonely
having nobody who wants to love him,
life sometimes sparkles like a kiss.

마음의 사막

별똥 하나가 성호를 긋고 지나간다
낙타 한 마리가 무릎을 꿇고 기도한 지는 이미 오래다
별똥은 무슨 죄가 그리 많아서 저리도 황급히 사라지고
낙타는 무슨 죄가 그리 많아서 평생을 무릎조차 펴지 못하는가
다시 별똥 하나가 성호를 긋고 지구 밖으로 떨어진다
위경련을 일으키며 멀리 녹두꽃 떨어지는 소리가 들린다
머리맡에 비수 한 자루 두고 잠이 드는 사막의 밤
초승달이 고개를 숙이고 시퍼렇게 칼을 갈고 앉아 있다
인생은 때때로 기도 속에 있지 않다
너의 영혼을 어루만지기 위해서는 침묵이 필요하다

The Heart's Desert

A shooting star crosses itself in passing.
It's been a long time since a camel knelt down and prayed.
What are the many sins that make the shooting star vanish so
    rapidly?
What are the many sins that make the camel unable to even bend
    a knee?
Again, a shooting star crosses itself as it falls away from the world.
The sound of a falling mung flower can be heard from far off,
provoking stomach cramps.
One desert night, laying a dagger by my pillow before falling asleep,
the crescent moon sits, head bowed, sharpening a sword.
At times human beings are not in prayer.
In order to soothe your soul, silence is necessary.

새벽 기도

이제는 홀로 밥을 먹지 않게 하소서
이제는 홀로 울지 않게 하소서
길이 끝나는 곳에 다시 길을 열어주시고
때로는 조그만 술집 희미한 등불 곁에서
추위에 떨게 하소서
밝음의 어둠과 깨끗함의 더러움과
배부름의 배고픔을 알게 하시고
아름다움의 추함과 희망의 절망과
기쁨의 슬픔을 알게 하시고
이제는 사랑하는 일을 두려워하지 않게 하소서
리어카를 끌고 스스로 밥이 되어
길을 기다리는 자의 새벽이 되게 하소서

Dawn Prayer

May I no longer eat alone now.
May I no longer weep alone now.
Where one road ends may a new road begin
and may I, from time to time, shiver with cold
beside the dim lamp of a tiny bar.
May I recognize the darkness in brightness,
the filth in purity, the hunger in repletion,
may I recognize the ugliness in beauty and the despair in hope,
the sorrow in joy.
May I no longer be afraid of loving now.
May I be the dawn of someone waiting for a path,
one who has turned himself into bread after drawing a cart.

모두 드리리

그대의 밥그릇에 내 마음의 첫눈을 담아 드리리
그대의 국그릇에 내 마음의 해골을 담아 드리리
나를 찔러 죽이고 강가에 버렸던 피묻은 칼 한 자루
강물에 씻어 다시 그대의 손아귀에 쥐어 드리리
아직도 죽여버리고 싶을 정도로 나를 사랑하는지
아직도 사랑하는 일보다 사랑하지 않는 일이 더 어려운지
미나리 다듬듯 내 마음의 뼈다귀들을 다듬어
그대의 차디찬 술잔 곁에 놓아 드리리
마지막 남은 한 방울 눈물까지도
말라버린 나의 검은 혓바닥까지도
그대의 식탁 위에 토막토막 잘라 드리리

I Will Give You All

I will fill your rice bowl with my heart's first snow.
I will fill your soup bowl with my heart's bones.
I will wash in the river and restore to your grasp the bloodstained
    sword
that killed me then lay thrown away by the riverside.
Maybe you still love me to the point of wanting to kill me;
maybe not loving is more difficult than loving;
I will trim my heart's bones as if trimming water parsley
then lay them beside your icy drinking glass.
Even my last remaining teardrop,
even my black, dried-up tongue
I will chop up and lay on your table.

당신에게

오늘도 당신의 밤하늘을 위해
나의 작은 등불을 끄겠습니다

오늘도 당신의 별들을 위해
나의 작은 촛불을 끄겠습니다

To You

Today, again, for your night sky
I will put out my little lamp.

Today, again, for your stars
I will put out my little candle.

까닭

내가 아직 한 포기 풀잎으로 태어나서
풀잎으로 사는 것은
아침마다 이슬을 맞이하기 위해서가 아니라
바짓가랑이를 적시며 나를 짓밟고 가는
너의 발자국을 견디기 위해서다

내가 아직 한 송이 눈송이로 태어나서
밤새껏 함박눈으로 내리는 것은
아침에 일찍 일어나 싸리빗자루로 눈길을 쓰시는
어머니를 위해서가 아니라
눈물도 없이 나를 짓밟고 가는
너의 발자국을 고이 남기기 위해서다

내가 아직도 쓸쓸히 노래 한 소절로 태어나서
밤마다 아리랑을 부르며 별을 바라보는 것은
너를 사랑하지 않아서가 아니라
너를 사랑하기엔
내 인생이 너무나 짧기 때문이다

Reasons

To be born as a clump of grass
and to yet live as grass
is not to greet the dew each morning,
but to endure your footsteps
as you trample over me, soaking your trouser-legs as you go.

To be born as a snowflake
and to yet fall in a blizzard all night long,
is not for Mother
who rises early in the morning and sweeps the snowy paths with
   a broom,
but to preserve your footprints
as you trample over me without a tear.

To be born lonely as a verse of a song
and to yet gaze at the stars every night singing "Arirang"
is not because I do not love you
but because my life is too short
to love you.

내 마음속의 마음이

내가 그대를 사랑하지 않는다면
지금 당장 내 목을 베어 가십시오
내가 그대를 사랑하지 않는다면
베어낸 내 목을
평생토록 베개로 삼아주십시오
그래도 내가 그대를 사랑하지 않는다면
다시 칼로 베개를 내려쳐주십시오
눈 내리는 그믐날 밤
기차역 부근에서
내 마음속의 마음이 말했습니다

The Heart inside My Heart

If I do not love you,
cut off my head at once.
If I do not love you
take my severed head
as your pillow
for all your life.
And if I still do not love you
again slash down at the pillow with your sword.
So spoke the heart inside my heart
near the railway station
one snowy night as another month ended.

기다림

내 그대가 그리워 제주도 만장굴로 걸어들어가
밤마다 그리움의 똥을 누고 용암기둥으로 높이 자라
만장굴 돌거북이 다시 바다로 유유히 헤엄쳐나갈 때까지
그대를 기다리고 또 기다립니다

Waiting

Yearning for you, I walk into Manjang Cave on Jeju Island,
every night I leave dumps of yearning that grow as high as
   a lava pillar,
and until the stone turtle in Manjang Cave again goes slowly
   swimming out to sea
I wait and wait for you.

새우잠

너를 기다리다가 해골이 되어
동해안 백사장에 버려져 있으리라
너를 사랑하다가 백골이 되어
어린 게들의 놀이터가 되리라
햇살이 지나간 다랑이논 같은 나는
너를 바라보는 것만으로
너의 운명이 되었으나
이제는 아무도 오가는 사람은 없어
동해안 바닷물을 다 들이켜리라
게들을 따라 봄날이 올 때까지
개펄 속에 들어가 새우잠을 자리라

Sleeping Curled like a Prawn

Turned into a skeleton after waiting for you
I'll end up discarded along the East Sea.
Turned into a skeleton after loving you
I'll turn into a playground for baby crabs.
Like a terraced rice field the sun has quit,
I became your destiny
simply as a gaze directed at you,
but now there is nobody coming or going
so I will gulp down all the water in the East Sea.
Until spring days come following the crabs
I will creep into the mudflats and sleep curled like a prawn.

끝끝내

헤어지는 날까지
사랑한다는 말 한마디 하지 못했습니다

헤어지는 날까지
차마
사랑한다는 말 한마디 하지 못했습니다

그대 처음과 같이 아름다울 줄을
그대 처음과 같이 영원할 줄을
헤어지는 날까지 알지 못하고

순결하게 무덤가에 무더기로 핀
흰 싸리꽃만 꺾어 바쳤습니다

사랑도 지나치면 사랑이 아닌 것을
눈물도 지나치면 눈물이 아닌 것을
헤어지는 날까지 알지 못하고

끝끝내 사랑한다는 말 한마디 하지 못했습니다
끝끝내 사랑한다는 말 한마디 하지 못했습니다

To the Bitter End

Until the day we parted
I was never once able to say I love you.

Until the day we parted,
alas,
I was never once able to say I love you.

Until the day we parted I never realized
you would still be as beautiful as at the start,
you would still be as eternal as at the start

I merely plucked and offered white bush clovers
blooming chastely in heaps beside a tomb.

Until the day we parted I never realized
if love passes it is not love,
if tears pass they are not tears.

To the bitter end I was never once able to say I love you.
To the bitter end I was never once able to say I love you.

첫키스에 대하여

내가 난생 처음으로 바라본 바다였다
희디흰 목덜미를 드러내고 끊임없이 달려오던 삼각파도였다
보지 않으려다 보지 않으려다 기어이 보고 만 수평선이었다
파도를 차고 오르는 갈매기떼들을 보며
나도 모르게 수평선 너머로 넘어지던 순간의 순간이었다
수평선으로 난 오솔길
여기저기 무더기로 피어난 해당화
그 붉은 꽃잎들의 눈물이었다

About My First Kiss

It was the sea, seen for the first time in my life.
There were triangular waves, rushing in endlessly,
exposing white necks.
It was the horizon I tried not to see, tried not to see, then saw.
As I watched flocks of seagulls go soaring up after skimming
    the waves,
it was the moment of time when I toppled beyond the horizon all
    unawares.
On the path arising from the horizon,
here and there saltspray roses blooming in mounds,
it was those crimson petals' tears

기적

수녀들이 날마다 강간을 당한다
술 취한 아버지를 아들이 칼로 찌르고 방에 불을 지르고
어머니가 발가벗고 아들에게 체위를 가르친다
아침마다 지하철은 개미들을 가득 싣고 한강으로 빠지고
개들이 고무신을 신고 낙엽을 밟으며 청와대 앞길을 걷는다
아버지도 딸의 옷을 벗기고 달 밝은 밤에 잠을 자지 않는다
머리에 물을 들인 소녀가 화장실 변기에 앉아
아이를 낳고 바람이 되어 사라진다
어디에도 인수봉은 보이지 않는다
내가 타고 갈 영구차 하나 백목련 아래로 느리게 지나간다
산등성이마다 포클레인들이 무덤을 파느라 분주하다

Miracles

Every day, Nuns suffer rape.
Sons stick knives into drunken fathers, set fire to rooms,
mothers strip, teach sons positions.
Every morning, subway trains fill with ants then topple into the
   Han River,
dogs go walking in front of the Blue House, trampling the fallen
   leaves, shod in rubber shoes.
Fathers, too, strip off daughters' clothes and do not sleep on bright
   moonlit nights.
A girl with dyed hair sits on the toilet,
gives birth, turns into wind and disappears.
The summit of Mount Bukhan is nowhere to be seen.
The hearse that will carry me passes slowly beneath magnolias.
On every mountain ridge mechanical diggers are busy
   digging graves.

거리에서

너를 사랑하는 날 거리에서 순대를 사먹는다
너를 사랑하는 날 소금에 순대를 찍어 먹으며
소금이 나의 눈물임을 기억한다

너와 이혼하는 날 거리에서 창녀를 만난다
창녀와 요강에 밥을 말아먹다가
팬티도 못 입은 채 다시 십자가에 매달린다

날이 흐르고 드디어 못질이 다 끝나고
흥건히 거리를 적시는 피를 보며
쓸쓸히 남근을 내려다본다

나도 이제 나를 속일 수 있는 놈이 되었다
굳이 봄을 기다릴 필요는 없다
거리엔 개들이 사람의 구두를 신고 다닌다

In the Street

The day I love you, I eat sliced blood sausage in the street.
The day I love you, as I dip the sausage slice in salt and eat it
I remember the salt is my tears.

The day I divorce you, I meet a hooker in the street.
After eating rice with the hooker from a chamberpot
once again I hang on the cross without any underwear.

The day goes by and when the nailing is finally over
as I gaze at the street soaked in blood,
forlornly, I look down at my prick.

At last I have become a wretch capable of fooling myself.
There's really no need to wait for spring.
In the street, dogs walk about wearing people's shoes.

등신불

강물도 없이 강이 흐르네
하늘도 없이 눈에 내리네
사랑도 없이 나는 살았네

모래를 삶아 밥을 해먹고
모래를 짜서 물을 마셨네

잘 가게
뒤돌아보지 말게
누구든 돌아보는 얼굴은 슬프네

눈이 오는 날
가끔 들리게

바람도 무덤이 없고
꽃들도 무덤이 없네

Life-Sized Buddha

No water, yet the river flows.
No sky, yet snow falls.
No love, yet I lived.

I ate rice made by boiling sand
and drank water made by squeezing sand.

Bye, now.
Don't look back.
Anyone's face looking back is sad.

On snowy days
come by now and then.

The wind has no grave, and
the flowers, too, have no graves.

배가 고프다

모래를 먹는다
배가 고프다
모래의 물을 마신다
목이 마르다

멍든 해당화의 손을 잡고
바닷가 기슭으로 기슭으로만 치달려도
배가 고프다

내가 얼마나 모래를 먹어야
바다가 될 수 있을까
내가 얼마나 모래를 먹어야
소금이 될 수 있을까

바위는 모래가 되어
제 이름이 없어지고
강물은 바다에 이르러
제 이름이 없어진다

모래를 먹는다
배가 고프다
다시 모래의 물을 마신다

I'm Hungry

I'm eating sand.
I'm hungry.
I'm drinking sand's water.
I'm thirsty.

Though I run to the shore, and only to the shore,
hand in hand with a bruised sweetbrier,
I'm hungry.

How much sand will I have to eat
to become the sea?
How much sand will I have to eat
to become salt?

When a rock is reduced to sand
it loses its name,
when a river reaches the sea
it loses its name.

I'm eating sand.
I'm hungry.
Again I'm drinking sand's water.

목이 마르다
오늘은 바다가 바늘구멍으로 들어가
나오지 않는다

I'm thirsty.

Today the sea has gone into the eye of a needle
and won't come out.

난(蘭) 앞에 엎드려 울다

해 뜨기 전
난(蘭) 앞에 엎드려 울다
강가에 나가 발을 씻고 돌아와
너부죽이 춘란 앞에 엎드려 울다
목련존자여
그대는 아직도
어머니를 위하여 울 수 있는가
망혼날 새벽
세상의 아침은 다시 오지 않고
춘란 향기는 보이지 않는데
목련존자여
적막강산에 어둠이 차다

I Weep Prostrate Before an Orchid

Before the sun rises
I weep prostrate before an orchid.
Returning from washing my feet at the river's side
I fall prostrate before a spring orchid and weep.
Venerable magnolia,
are you still able
to weep for your mother?
Early on the day of the dead
the world's morning fails to dawn,
the spring orchid's scent cannot be seen,
venerable magnolia,
this wasteland is full of darkness.

외나무다리

둥근 달이 떠 있다
짐을 내려놓아라
푸른 별이 떠 있다
길을 건너라

그대와 나의 깊은 계곡
팽나무로 만든 외나무다리 위를
반가사유상이 괴었던 손을 내리고
조심조심 걸어서 간다

짐을 내려놓아라
무겁지 않느냐
눈물을 내려놓아라
마르지 않느냐

A Single Log Bridge

The round moon has risen.
Lay down your load.
A blue star has risen.
Cross the path.

Over the single hackberry log bridge
across the deep valley of me and you
lowering my pensive bodhisattva hand
cautiously, cautiously I advance.

Lay down your load.
Isn't it heavy?
Lay aside your tears.
Have they not yet dried?

망경사(望鏡寺)

눈 내리는 태백산을 오른다
눈길에 난 새들의 발자국을 따라
가파른 피나무 숲길을 오른다
사랑하는 사람은 어디 있는가
아직도 너의 피묻은 종소리는 들리지 않고
새들이 걸어간 하늘가에
새똥처럼 망경사가 버려져 있다
오늘도 너를 용서하기 위하여
나를 먼저 용서하는 일은 괴로운 일이다
오늘도 너를 만나기 위하여
절벽 위에 뿌리를 내리는 일은 괴로운 일이다
한차례 눈은 내렸다가 또 그친다
눈길에 누고 간 사람의 똥보다
새들의 똥이 더 아름답다

Manggyeongsa Temple

I climb Mount Taebaek as snow is falling.
Following the footprints of birds in the snow
I climb the steep path through a linden tree grove.
Where is the one I love?
As yet your bloodstained bell cannot be heard
and Manggyeongsa Temple lies abandoned like bird droppings
at the rim of the sky where the birds have gone walking.
Having to forgive myself first
in order to forgive you again today is a painful task.
Putting down roots on the edge of a cliff
in order to meet you again today is a painful task.
Snow falls, then stops.
On the snowy path, the droppings of the birds
are more beautiful than those left by any human.

Part 3

결빙

결빙의 순간은 뜨겁다
꽝꽝 얼어붙은 겨울강
도도히 흐르는 강물조차
일생에 한번은
모든 흐름을 멈추고
서로 한몸을 이루는
순간은 뜨겁다

Icebound

The moment ice forms is a hot one.
The winter river is frozen hard.
That moment when even rushing streams
for once in a lifetime
cease all their flowing
and become a single body
is a hot one.

허공

어머니 바느질하시다가
바늘로 허공을 찌른다
피가 난다
어머니 바늘로 허공을 기워
수의를 만드신다

Air

As Mother sews
she pricks the air with her needle.
Blood oozes out.
Mother mends the air with her needle
to make a shroud.

밥값

어머니
아무래도 제가 지옥에 한번 다녀오겠습니다
아무리 멀어도
아침에 출근하듯이 갔다가
저녁에 퇴근하듯이 다녀오겠습니다
식사 거르지 마시고 꼭꼭 씹어서 잡수시고
외출하실 때는 가스불 꼭 잠그시고
너무 염려하지는 마세요
지옥도 사람 사는 곳이겠지요
지금이라도 밥값을 하러 지옥에 가면
비로소 제가 인간이 될 수 있을 겁니다

Earning my Keep

Mother,
I think I'll go pay a visit to Hell.
No matter how far away,
I'll set off as if leaving for work in the morning
then come back as if getting off work in the evening.
Don't skip meals, chew your food well before swallowing,
be sure to turn off the gas when you step out,
and don't worry too much about me.
Hell, too, must be a place where people live,
so if I go to Hell to earn my keep
at last I'll be able to become a human being.

부활

진달래 핀
어느 봄날에
돌멩이 하나 주워 손바닥에 올려놓았다
돌멩이가 처음에는
참새 한 마리 가쁜 숨을 쉬듯이
가쁘게 숨을 몰아쉬더니
차차 시간이 지나자 잠이라도 든 듯
고른 숨을 내쉬었다
내가 봄 햇살을 맞으며
엄마 품에 안겨
숨을 쉬듯이

Resurrection

One spring day
when azaleas were in bloom,
I picked up a pebble and held it in my palm.
At first the pebble
breathed quickly
like a sparrow panting
but after a while it began to breathe evenly
as if it had fallen asleep,
like me breathing,
snuggled against my mother's breast
bathed in spring sunshine.

모유

어미 잃은
배고픈 갓난 강아지 몇 마리
이웃집 늙은 암캐의 품에 안겨주자
이튿날
암캐의 젖멍울이 모두 서고
하얀 젖이 흘러나왔다
강아지들은 하루 종일
그 젖을 빨아먹고
꼬물꼬물
웃으면서 기어다녔다

Mother's Milk

A few hungry newborn puppies
that had lost their mother
were taken to the bosom of the old dog next door.
The following day
her teats were swollen
and white milk began to emerge.
The pups sucked at the milk
all day long, and,
wriggling
crawled about laughing.

천사

천사는 손바닥에도 눈이 있다
발바닥에도 눈이 있다
이마에도 눈이 있다
온몸이 다 눈동자다

Angels

Angels have eyes on the palms of their hands
they have eyes on the soles of their feet
they have eyes on their foreheads
their whole body is an eye.

고비

고비 사막에 가지 않아도
나는 늘 고비에 간다
영원히 살 것처럼 꿈꾸고
내일 죽을 것처럼 살면서
오늘도 죽을 고비를 겨우 넘겼다
이번이 마지막 고비다

Crossing

Even without crossing the Gobi desert
I am crossing it all the time.
While dreaming as though I'll live forever,
living as though I'll die tomorrow,
today again I nearly died as I crossed.
This is the final crossing.

인삼밭을 지나며

내 어찌 인간을 닮고 싶었으랴
내 일찍이 풀의 이름으로 태어나
어찌 인간의 이름을 닮고 싶었으랴
나는 하늘의 풀일 뿐
들풀일 뿐
어찌 인간의 영혼을 지녔으랴
어찌 인간이 되고 싶었으랴

Passing a Ginseng Field

Why did I want to be like a human?
I was born under the name of a plant.
Why did I want to have a name like a human?
I am just one of heaven's plants,
just one wild plant.
How could I have a human soul?
How could I want to become human?

물의 꽃

펄펄 끓는 물에
꽃이 핀다
오직 한 사람을 위하여
그 꽃을 꺾어
꽃다발을 만든다
사랑하는 일을
두려워하지 않기 위하여
펄펄 끓는 물에
꽃은 다시 깊게
뿌리를 내린다

Flower in Water

In boiling water
a flower blooms.
I pluck that flower
and make a bouquet
for just one person.
So as to not be afraid
of loving,
once again the flower
puts down deep roots
in boiling water.

투우

나의 뿔은 풀이다
너의 뿔도 풀이다
머리통을 맞대고
날카롭게 비녀뿔을 치켜세우고
불타는 석양이 깃든 저 눈빛
어리석다
분노는 풀과 같은 것
인간을 위하여
더이상 싸우고 싶지 않다
넓은 앞가슴과
강한 다리의 힘을 풀고
서로 껴안고
낮잠이나 푹 자고 싶다

Bullfight

My horns are grass
your horns, too, are grass.
Head to head
sharp hairpin horns raised
the eyes full of a sunset blaze
are stupid.
Anger is like grass.
I no longer want to fight
for people.
Letting go of the tension in the broad breast
and strong legs
I simply want us to doze soundly,
embracing each other.

설해목(雪害木)

천년 바람 사이로
고요히
폭설이 내릴 때
내가 폭설을 너무 힘껏 껴안아
내 팔이 뚝뚝 부러졌을 뿐
부러져도 그대로 아름다울 뿐
아직
단 한번도 폭설에게
상처받은 적 없다

Snow-Damaged Trees

When a blizzard falls
quietly
amidst gusts of ancient wind
I embrace the blizzard so strongly
that my arms break
and even if they break they are still as beautiful.
I have, as yet, not once
been wounded
by a blizzard.

거울

거울을 보다가 가끔
내 얼굴이 악마의 얼굴이 아닌가
한참 들여다볼 때가 있다
거울이 가끔 내 얼굴을
와장창
깨뜨려버릴 때가 있다

A Mirror

Sometimes when I look in the mirror
I wonder if my face is that of a demon
and I stare at it for quite a while.
Sometimes the mirror
shatters
my face to bits.

어느 벽보판 앞에서

어느 벽보판 앞
현상수배범 전단지 사진 속에
내 얼굴이 있었다
안경을 끼고 입꼬리가 축 처진 게
영락없이 내 얼굴이었다
내가 무슨 대죄를 지어
나도 모르게 수배되고 있는지 몰라
벽보판 앞을 평생을 서성이다가
마침내 알았다
당신을 사랑하지 않은 죄
당신을 사랑하지 않고
늙어버린 죄

Standing before a Notice Board

Standing before a notice board,
in the photo on a "Wanted" poster
I saw my face.
Wearing glasses, the corners of the mouth drooping
it was definitely my face.
I did not know what great crime I had committed
so that I, for reasons unknown to myself, had become a wanted man
and I lingered a lifetime before the notice board
until I finally realized,
it was for the crime of not loving you,
the crime of having grown old
without loving you.

꽃

사람은 꽃을 꺾어도
꽃은 사람을 꺾지 않는다
사람은 꽃을 버려도
꽃은 사람을 버리지 않는다
영정 속으로 사람이 기어들어가
울고 있어도
꽃은 손수건을 꺼내
밤새도록
장례식장 영정의 눈물을 닦아준다

Flowers

Though people pick flowers
flowers never pick people.
Though people trash flowers
flowers never trash people.
Though people go crawling into a funeral photo
and weep
flowers produce handkerchiefs
and all night long
wipe away the tears of the photo in the funeral hall.

별들은 울지 않는다

자살하지 마라
별들은 울지 않는다
비록 지옥 말고는 아무 데도
갈 데가 없다 할지라도
자살하지 마라
천사도 가끔 자살하는 이의 손을
놓쳐버릴 때가 있다
별들도 가끔 너를
바라보지 못할 때가 있다

Stars Don't Cry

Do not kill yourself.
Stars won't cry.
Even if you feel that you have nowhere to go
except Hell
do not kill yourself.
There are times when even angels lose their grip
on the hands of people killing themselves.
And there are times when even stars
cannot look at you.

새똥

천사의 가슴에도
똥이 들어 있다
하하하
새똥이 들어 있다

Bird Shit

Even angels' breasts
are full of shit.
Ha ha ha.
Full of bird shit.

물의 신발

비가 온다
집이 떠내려간다
살짝 방문을 열고
신발을 방 안에 들여놓는다
비가 그치지 않는다
신발이 떠내려간다
나는 이제 나의 마지막 신발을 따라
바다로 간다
멸치떼가 기다리는 바다의
수평선이 되어
수평선 위로 치솟는 고래가 되어
너를 기다린다

The Water's Shoes

Rain is falling.
Houses are being swept away.
I open the door slightly
and bring my shoes inside.
The rain does not stop.
Shoes are being swept away.
Following my last pair of shoes,
now I am headed seaward.
I become the horizon
of the sea where shoals of anchovies await,
become a whale soaring above the horizon,
and wait for you.

짐

내 짐 속에는 다른 사람의 짐이 절반이다
다른 사람의 짐을 지고 가지 않으면
결코 내 짐마저 지고 갈 수 없다
길을 떠날 때마다
다른 사람의 짐은 멀리 던져버려도
어느새 다른 사람의 짐이
내가 짊어지고 가는 짐의 절반 이상이다
풀잎이 이슬을 무거워하지 않는 것처럼
나도 내 짐이 아침이슬이길 간절히 바랐으나
이슬에도 햇살의 무게가 절반 이상이다
이제 짐을 내려놓고 별을 바라본다
지금까지 버리지 않고 지고 온 짐덩이 속에
내 짐이 남아 있는 것은 아무것도 없다
내가 비틀거리며 기어이 짊어지고 온
다른 사람의 짐만 남아 있다

Burdens

Half of my burden is made up of other people's burdens.
If I do not shoulder other people's burdens,
I will never be able to shoulder my own burden and travel on,
Even if I hurl other people's burdens far away
every time I set out,
before I know it more than half the burden weighing me down
is other people's burdens.
Just as a blade of grass does not find dew burdensome,
I, too, had earnestly hoped that my burden would be light as
    morning dew,
but more than half the weight of dew is sunlight.
Now I lay down my burden and look up at the stars.
In the bundled burden I have so far carried and not cast aside
nothing at all of my own burden is left.
All that remains is other people's burdens that I bore at last,
stumbling as I went along the way.

충분한 불행

나는 이미 충분히 불행하다
불행이라도 충분하므로
혹한의 겨울이 찾아오는 동안
많은 것을 잃었지만 모든 것을 잃지는 않았다
죽음이란 보고 싶을 때 보지 못하는 것
보지 못하지만 살아갈수록 함께 살아가는 것
더러운 물에 깨끗한 물을 붓지 못하고
깨끗한 물에 더러운 물을 부으며 살아왔지만
나의 눈물은 뜨거운 바퀴가 되어
차가운 겨울 거리를 굴러다닌다
남의 불행에서 위로를 받았던 나의 불행이
이제 남의 불행에게 위로가 되는 시간
밤늦게 시간이 가득 든 검은 가방을 들고
종착역에 내려도
아무 데도 전화할 데가 없다

Enough Unhappiness

I am already unhappy enough.
Because at least my unhappiness is enough,
even as bitter cold winter draws near
I have lost many things but did not lose everything.
Death cannot be seen when I want to see it.
Though it cannot be seen, the longer I live the more it lives with me.
Unable to pour clean water into dirty water,
I have spent my life pouring dirty water into clean water.
Even so, my tears have become hot wheels
rolling about the cold winter streets.
Now, it is time that my unhappiness,
once comforted by others' unhappiness,
should become a comfort for others' unhappiness.
Late in the evening, I alight at the last stop,
carrying a black bag full of time,
but there is no one to whom I can make a call.

바닥에 쏟은 커피를 바라보며

바닥에 쏟은 커피는 바닥이 잔이다
바닥에 커피를 쏟으면
커피는 순간 검은 구름이 된다
바다가 비에 젖지 않고 비를 바다로 만들듯
바닥도 커피에 젖지 않고 커피를 바닥으로 만든다
바닥을 걷는 흉측한 발들아
물 위를 걸은 예수의 흉내를 내다가 익사한 발들아
검은 구름떼가 흘러가는 바닥의 잔을 들어라
오늘도 바닥의 잔을 높이 들고
남은 인생의 첫날인 오늘보다
남은 인생의 마지막 날인 내일을 생각하며
봄비 내리는 창가를 서성거려라

On Looking at Coffee Spilled on the Floor

For coffee spilled on the floor, the floor is its cup.
If I spill coffee on the floor,
in a flash the coffee becomes a black cloud.
Just as the sea is not soaked by rain but turns the rain into sea,
the floor is not soaked by coffee but turns the coffee into floor.
You, ugly feet walking over the floor.
You, feet that drowned while imitating Jesus walking on water.
Raise aloft the floor-cup where black clouds float past.
Lift high the floor-cup once again today, and,
thinking less of today, the first day of the rest of your life,
and more of tomorrow, the last day of the rest of your life,
hover by the window as the spring rain falls.

죄송합니다

아직 숟가락을 들고 있어서 죄송합니다
도대체 뭘 얻어먹을 게 있다고
해는 지는데
숟가락을 들고 하루 종일
지하철을 헤매고 다녀서 죄송합니다
살얼음 낀 한강에 떠다니는 청둥오리들
우두커니 바라보아서 죄송합니다
한강대교 위에서 하늘로 힘껏 던진 돌멩이들
별이 되지 못해서 죄송합니다
믿음이 없으면서도 그분의 옷자락에 손을 대고
그분의 신발에 입맞추어서 죄송합니다
진주조개를 돌로 내리쳐서
채 만들어지지도 않은 진주를 꺼낸 일도 죄송합니다
겨울비 내리는 서울역 뒷골목
오늘도 흰구름이 찾아오지 않아서 죄송합니다
언제나 시작도 없이 끝만 있어서 죄송합니다

I'm Sorry

I'm sorry I'm still carrying a spoon.
I'm sorry I spent the whole day
wandering about the subway carrying a spoon,
desperately hoping for something to eat,
and now the sun is setting.
I'm sorry for staring blankly
at ducks afloat on the thin ice covering the Han River.
I'm sorry the pebbles I tossed up at the sky from the Han River
    Bridge
could not turn into stars.
I'm sorry that, although I do not have faith, I touched the fringe of
    His garment
and kissed His shoes.
I'm sorry for smashing oyster shells with a stone
and taking out pearls yet to be fully formed.
I'm sorry that today, again, no white clouds visited
the back alleys at Seoul Station where the winter rain fell.
I'm sorry there are always only ends and no beginnings.

왼쪽에 대한 편견

한쪽 날개가 왼쪽으로 약간 기울어진 채
겨울 하늘을 나는 청둥오리가 더 아름답다
한쪽 어깨가 왼쪽으로 약간 기울어진 채 걸어가는 사람의
뒷모습이 더 아름답다
나는 젊은 마음의 육체를 지녔을 때부터 왼쪽 길로만 걸어가
지금 외로운 마음의 육체마저도 왼쪽으로 더 기울어졌다
직선의 대로이거나 어두운 골목이거나
내가 바라보던 모든 수평선도 지평선도 왼쪽으로 더 기울어졌다
기울어진다는 것은 아름다워진다는 것이다
기울어진다는 것은 사랑한다는 것이다
나는 지금도 멀리 사람을 바라볼 때
꼭 왼쪽에서 바라본다
왼쪽에서 바라본 사람의 옆모습이 가장 아름답다

Prejudice Regarding the Left

A wild duck that flies across the winter sky
with one wing tilted slightly to the left is more beautiful.
The back of a person walking
with one shoulder tilting slightly to the left is more beautiful.
From the days when my body had a youthful heart
I always only took the left-hand path
and now, even that body with a lonely heart has tilted more to
 the left.
Be it a straight highway or a dark alley,
all the horizons I've gazed at have tilted more to the left.
To say something is tilting is to say it is growing beautiful.
To say something is tilting is to say you love it.
Still now, were I to gaze at someone from far away
I would always gaze from the left.
The side view of someone seen from the left is the most beautiful
 of all.

바다의 성자

이제 알겠다
내가 술안주로 북북 찢어먹은 북어가
명태의 미라인 것을
그동안 즐겨먹은 안동 간고등어도
바짝 마른 멸치도
고등어의 미라
멸치의 미라인 것을
돈과 사람을 구분하지 못하고
허둥지둥 살아오는 동안
멸치가 게워놓은 바다도 보지 못하고
명태가 토해놓은 파도소리도 듣지 못하고
이제 알겠다
더이상 인간에게서
성자가 나오지 않는 까닭을
그들이야말로
바다의 성자라는 것을

The Sea's Saints

Now I realize:
the dried fish I tore apart to accompany my drinks
is mummified pollock;
the Andong salt mackerel I've so far enjoyed,
and the crispy dried anchovies
are mummified mackerel,
mummified anchovies.
While I've been rushing on through life,
unable to distinguish money and men,
I could not see the sea thrown up by anchovies,
nor hear the waves vomited up by mackerels.
Now I realize:
the reason why there are no more saints
emerging among men
is that those
are the sea's very saints.

Part 4

폐사지처럼 산다

요즘 어떻게 사느냐고 묻지 마라
폐사지처럼 산다
요즘 뭐하고 지내느냐고 묻지 마라
폐사지에 쓰러진 탑을 일으켜세우며 산다
나 아직 진리의 탑 하나 세운 적 없지만
죽은 친구의 마음 사리 하나 넣어둘
부도탑 한번 세운 적 없지만
폐사지에 처박혀 나뒹구는 옥개석 한 조각
부둥켜안고 산다
가끔 웃으면서 라면도 끓여먹고
바람과 풀도 뜯어먹고
부서진 석등에 불이나 켜며 산다
부디 어떻게 사느냐고 다정하게 묻지 마라
너를 용서하지 못하면 내가 죽는다고
거짓말도 자꾸 진지하게 하면
진지한 거짓말이 되는 일이 너무 부끄러워
입도 버리고 혀도 파묻고
폐사지처럼 산다

Living like a Ruined Temple

Don't ask how I'm faring these days;
I'm living like a ruined temple.
Don't ask what I am doing these days;
I live re-erecting pagodas in a ruined temple.
I have yet to erect one pagoda of truth,
have never once been able to build a stupa
to enshrine the relic of a dead friend's heart,
but I live stuck in a ruined temple
clinging onto a piece of scattered roof stone.
Sometimes I live, smiling, as I boil some instant noodles to eat,
or pluck and eat some wind or grass
and I light lamps in broken stone lanterns.
Do not, please, ask kindly how life is going.
If I keep lying gravely,
saying I will die if I cannot forgive you,
turning into grave lies is so shameful
that I live like a ruined temple,
casting away my mouth, burying my tongue.

도망자

어느 봄날
내 책상 위에 놓인
십자고상에 매달려 있던 사내가 내려와
내 손에 못을 박는다
내 발에 못을 박는다
나는 밤새도록 도망치다가
그 사내한테 다시 붙잡혀
그 사내 대신 십자가에 매달려 운다
목이 마르다
병든 노모는 보이지 않는다
새벽별들을 거느리고
황소 한 마리 말없이 다가와
내 야윈 잔등을 쓸어주다가
빙그레 웃는다

Runaway

One spring day
the man attached to the cross
on the wall above my desk comes down,
drives nails into my hands,
drives nails into my feet.
All night long I flee
then, once he has caught me again,
I weep, hanging on the cross instead of him.
I thirst.
There is no sign of that sick old mother.
Leading the dawn stars,
an ox approaches quietly,
strokes my emaciated back
and smiles.

종이코끼리

온몸이 텅 빈
종이코끼리를 타고 길을 걷는다
아기부처님을 태우고 묵묵히
연등행렬을 따라가던 종이코끼리 한 마리
코가 잘려나간 채 종로 뒷골목에 버려져 있어
코 없는 종이코끼리를 타고 길을 걷는다
아직 남아 있는 살아가야 할 날들을 위하여
바람이 가장 강하게 부는 날 새들이 집을 짓듯이
폭풍우가 가장 강하게 몰아치는 날
이 순간의 너와집 한 채 지어 불을 지핀다
버리지 않으면 살아갈 수 없으므로
살아가기 위해서는 누구나 버려야 하므로
온몸이 텅 빈 흰 종이코끼리 한 마리 불태워
한줌 재를 뿌린다

A Paper Elephant

I travel along the road, riding on a paper elephant
with a body completely hollow.
There was a paper elephant that had silently carried a baby Buddha
in the lotus lantern parade
lying abandoned with its trunk cut off
in a Jong-ro back alley,
so I am traveling along atop a trunk-less paper elephant.
For the days still left to be lived,
just as birds build their nests on days when the wind is strongest,
when storms rage at their wildest,
I build this moment's shingle-roofed house, then set it alight.
Since life is not possible without discarding,
since everyone has to discard in order to live,
I set fire to the hollow paper elephant
and scatter a handful of ashes.

사랑할 원수가 없어서 슬프다

어느 가을날
시신 없는 영결미사에 참석하고 돌아와
내가 살아온 삶과
내가 살고 싶은 삶 사이에다 침을 뱉었다
내가 고통받을 때마다
하느님도 고통받는다는 사실이 부담스러워
내가 거역했던 운명과
내가 받아들였던 숙명 사이에다 오줌을 갈겼다
그리고 하루 종일 낙엽을 따라 걸었다
개미 한 마리
내 뒤를 따르다가 별을 쳐다본다
나는 오늘도
사랑할 원수가 없어서 슬프다

Sad, Having No Enemy to Love

One autumn day,
returning home from a requiem mass without a corpse,
I spat into the gap between the life I have lived
and the life I want to live.
Burdened by the fact that whenever I suffer
God suffers too,
I peed freely into the gap between the destiny I have disobeyed
and the fate I have accepted.
Then I walked the streets all day long, following the fallen leaves.
One ant,
after following me about, stares up at the stars.
Today again I am
sad, having no enemy to love.

희방폭포

이대로 당신 앞에 서서 죽으리
당신의 사리(舍利)로 밥을 해먹고
당신의 눈물로 술을 마신 뒤
희방사(喜方寺) 앞마당에 수국으로 피었다가
꽃잎이 질 때까지 묵언정진하고 나서
이대로 서서 죽어 바다로 가리

Huibang Falls

Standing thus before you, I will die.
After eating rice made of your ashes
and drinking wine composed of your tears,
then blossoming as a hydrangea in the front yard of
  Huibangsa Temple
I will observe a rule of total silence until the petals drop,
then, standing thus, I will die and head for the sea.

실크로드

발 없이 걸어서 간다
무릎 없이 기어서 간다
배가 고파 낙타의 똥을 먹는다
낙타가 내 얼굴에 침을 뱉는다
길 잃은 쌍봉낙타여
천산북로(天山北路)는 어디인가
달은 뜨지 않고 목이 마르다
전생에 그대와 나를 잇는 비단길 하나 있었던가
삶도 없이 죽음에 이르게 될까봐 두려워라
언제나 비극이 오는 것을 알았지만
막을 수는 없었다
나는 한낱 짐승일 뿐
눈물의 짐승일 뿐
짐승처럼 그대를 사랑했을 뿐
길 잃은 쌍봉낙타여
천산(天山)으로 가는 길은
보이지 않는다

Silk Road

I walk on with no feet.
I crawl on with no knees.
Hungry, I eat a camel's dung.
The camel spits in my face.
Ah, Bactrian camel gone astray,
where is the route to the north of Tian Shan?
The moon does not rise and I am thirsty.
I eat more red sand.
In a previous existence, was there a silk road linking you and me?
Fear reaching death without having lived.
I always knew tragedy was coming
but could not prevent it.
I am a mere animal,
merely an animal of tears,
I merely loved you like an animal,
Bactrian camel gone astray,
The road to Tian- Shan
cannot be seen.

서귀포에서

바람이 차다 창문을 닫아라
서귀포의 어둠도 추위에 떨고 있다
흐르던 폭포도 굶주림에 얼어붙는
아귀도의 눈보라가 휘몰아치고 있다

창문을 닫아라 두려움은 없다
두려움 끝에 오는 적막이 두려울 뿐
적막 끝에 오는 슬픔이 두려울 뿐
내가 가장 두려워했던 건 사랑일 뿐
세상은 나를 필요로 할 때만 사랑했을 뿐

어둠이 차다 창문을 닫아라
서귀포 앞바다의 비명소리가 들린다
저기 저 동백 꽃잎 한 점이
눈보라에 숨을 거둔다

In Seoguipo

The wind is cold. Shut the window.
Seoguipo's darkness, too, is trembling with the cold.
The waterfall that once flowed, the snowstorms
in the realm of hungry ghosts, frozen with huger, rage on.

Shut the window. I have no fear.
I fear only the silence that comes at the end of fear,
I fear only the sorrow that comes at the end of silence,
the thing I used to fear most of all was love,
The world only loved me when it needed me.

The darkness is cold. Shut the window.
I can hear the screams from the sea before Seoguipo.
Out there one camellia petal
is dying in the blizzard.

감포에서

작살나무는 작살이 났습니다
님나무는 님을 잃었습니다
멸치는 멸치똥으로만 남았습니다
감은사 돌탑도 무너져내렸습니다
술을 마시든지 아예 침묵하십시오
죽음이 모든 것을 용서해주지는 않습니다
비극이 오는 것을 알았지만
막을 수는 없었습니다
갈매기 한 마리가
수평선을 끊어놓고 사라집니다

In Gampo

A beautyberry tree gave birth to beauty.
A bead tree lost its beads.
Anchovies remained only as anchovy guts.
The stone wall at Gameunsa Temple collapsed.
Either drink or just remain silent.
Death does not forgive everything.
I knew tragedy was coming
but could not prevent it.
One seagull
severs the horizon and vanishes.

첫눈 오는 날

나는 죽으면 첫눈 오는 날
겨울 하늘을 날다 지친 새들 앞에서
영혼결혼식을 올리고 싶었다
하객들로 새들을 모셔놓고
어머니가 새들에게 모이를 주고 있을 때
진정으로 사랑하는 한 여자와
영혼결혼식을 올리고 싶었다
눈 속에 찬 매화는
아직 홀로 향기를 토하지 못하고
가섭은 부처님이 꽃을 들어도 미소 짓지 않으나
내 언젠가 첫눈 오는 날
새들을 모시고 영혼결혼식을 올리면
여름날 소나기 한차례 지나간 뒤
부석사 앞마당에 핀 접시꽃 한 송이 꺾어
내 영혼을 축하해주십시오

The Day Snow First Falls

When I die, on the day snow first falls
I wanted to celebrate a soul-marriage
before the birds weary from flying across the winter sky.
Summoning the birds as guests
when Mother is giving the birds their feed
I wanted to celebrate a soul-marriage
with a woman I truly loved.
One plum blossom cold in the snow
is as ever unable to emit fragrance alone
and though Buddha holds up a flower, Kasyapa does not smile,
but always, on the day snow first falls,
inviting the birds, as I celebrate a soul-marriage
once a summer day's shower has passed
pluck a hollyhock blossoming in front of Buseoksa Temple
and congratulate my soul.

칼날

칼날 위를 걸어서 간다
한걸음 한걸음 내디딜 때마다
피는 나지 않는다
눈이 내린다
보라
칼날과 칼날 사이로
겨울이 지나가고
개미가 지나간다
칼날 위를 맨발로 걷기 위해서는
스스로 칼날이 되는 길뿐
우리는 희망 없이도 열심히 살 수 있다

Blades

I am walking on blades.
As I walk along, step by step,
I do not bleed.
Snow is falling.
Look.
Between one blade and the next
winter is passing,
an ant is passing.
The only way to walk barefoot on blades
is to become a blade myself.
Even without hope, we can still live intensely.

갈대는 새벽에 울지 않는다

새벽 종소리가 들리는 사하촌(寺下村)에 첫눈이 내린다
산죽(山竹) 잎새에 하얗게 내려앉은 함박눈이 벼랑 아래로 떨어진다
어머니를 찾아가는 눈길에 붉은 피가 번진다
사람들이 손에 쥔 칼을 버리고 길을 떠난다
나는 마른 강가의 갈대숲에 나가
너를 기다리다가 다시 서서 죽는다
무심히 눈송이가 쌓인다
갈대는 새벽에 울지 않는다

Reeds Do Not Weep at Dawn

In the village below the temple, from where the dawn bell can
    be heard,
the first snow is falling.
The snow settling white on bamboo leaves goes tumbling over a cliff.
On the snowy path taken in search of Mother red blood spreads.
People throw aside the knives they are clasping and quit the path.
I go out to the bed of reeds beside the dry stream
and wait for you, then, still standing, die.
Indifferently, snowflakes go piling high.
Reeds do not weep at dawn.

슬프다 구주 오셨네

슬프다 구주 오셨네
새벽에 똥이나 누고 나와 맞으라
슬프다 구주 오셨네
배추밭에 똥거름이나 뿌리고 나와 맞으라

슬프다 구주 오셨네
개 밥그릇에 밥이나 퍼주고 나와 맞으라
슬프다 구주 오셨네
푸른 시냇물에 성기나 씻고 나와 맞으라

엉덩이보다 배꼽을 흔들며
장미꽃보다 작약을 흔들며
죽은 애인의 손을 잡고 나와 맞으라
똥 친 막대기나 되어 잠이 들어라

Grief to the World, the Savior Has Come.

Grief to the world,, the Savior has come.
After pooping at daybreak, come out and greet him.
Grief to the world, the Savior has come.
After spreading dung on the cabbage patch, come out and greet him.

Grief to the world, the Savior has come.
After spooning rice into the dog's feeding bowl, come out and greet him.
Grief to the world, the Savior has come.
After washing your genitals in an azure stream, come out and greet him.

Waving your navel rather than your bottom,
waving a peony rather than a rose,
holding your dead lover by the hand, come out and greet him.
Turn into a shit stick and go to sleep.

선운사 상사화

선운사 동백꽃은 너무 바빠
보러 가지 못하고
선운사 상사화는 보러 갔더니
사랑했던 그 여자가 앞질러가네
그 여자 한번씩 뒤돌아볼 때마다
상사화가 따라가다 발걸음을 멈추고
나도 얼른 돌아서서
나를 숨겼네

Spider Lilies at Seonunsa Temple

I was too busy to go and see
the camellias at Seonunsa
so I went to see Seonunsa's spider lilies,
only to see the woman I'd loved walk past me.
Every time she looked back
the lilies following her stopped in their footsteps
and I, too, quickly turned back
and hid.

수덕여관

일생에 한번쯤
수덕사 수덕여관에 여장을 풀고
평생 오지 않았던 잠을 자보아라
열매 맺지 않는 꽃이 붉은 열매를 맺을 것이다
비록 이튿날 아침 깨어나지 못한다 하더라도
일생에 하룻밤쯤
수덕여관 산당화에 기대어 잠을 자보아라
열매 맺지 않는 꽃이 맺은 열매에
다시 붉은 꽃이 피는 것을 볼 수 있을 것이다
그래도 평생 오지 않는 잠이 있다면
수덕여관 샘물을 한 바가지 들이켜보아라
물 위에 코끼리를 타고
모든 쓸쓸한 사랑이 지나가버린다

Sudeok Inn

Just once in a lifetime
take off your traveling clothes in Sudeok Inn by Sudeoksa Temple
and sleep a sleep such as has never once come in your life.
Flowers bearing no fruit will yield red fruit.
Even if you are unable to wake up the next morning,
for one night in a lifetime
sleep propped against the flowering quince tree at Sudeok Inn.
You will be able to see red flowers blooming again
on the fruit yielded by the flowers that bear no fruit.
If still there is a sleep that has never yet come in your lifetime,
drink a bowl of Sudeok Inn's spring water.
Riding an elephant on the water,
all your melancholy love will go drifting away.

웃음

개심사에 다녀온 뒤
아파트 베란다에 풍경을 달아놓고
풍경소리가 들리기를 기다린다
아무리 기다려도 들리지 않는다
어머니가 돌아가셔도 들리지 않는다
하루는 손으로 툭 쳐서
개심사 해우소 가을 지붕 위에 떨어지는
노란 은행잎 소리 같은
풍경소리를 내어보고
그냥 혼자 웃는다

A Smile

After visiting Gaesimsa Temple
I hung a wind-bell on my apartment balcony
and waited to hear it chime.
I waited and waited and heard not a sound.
Even when Mother died it did not chime.
One day I struck it with my hand,
producing a chime
like the sound of a yellow gingko leaf
falling on the autumn roof of the Gaesimsa toilet,
and just smiled to myself.

심우장에 가다

성북동에 봄이 와서
심우장에 가다
황급히 신발을 벗고
영정에 향을 올리고
집안 구석구석을 살피며
소를 찾는다
소는 없고
향나무에 푸른 고삐만 매여 있다
나는 고삐를 풀어 손에 꼭 쥐고
당신이 타고 가신
소를 찾아
성북동 골목을 평생 돌아다닌다
달이 뜬다
소똥 봐라 소리치며
동네아이들이 졸졸 따라온다
멀리서 당신인가
워낭소리 들린다

Visit to Simujang*

Spring has come to Seongbuk-dong
so I set off to visit Simujang.
Hurriedly removing my shoes
I offer incense before the portrait
then explore every nook and cranny of the house
searching for the ox.
There is no sign of the ox,
only the green bridle tied to a juniper tree.
Untying the bridle and clasping it tight in my hands
I spend a whole lifetime roaming the alleys of Seongbuk-dong
in search of the ox
that you rode away on.
The moon rises.
The neighborhood children trail along behind me
shouting: Look at the ox-dung.
Is that you? From far away
I hear an ox-bell ringing.

---

* Simujang is the house in northern Seoul where the poet and independence fighter Manhae Han Yong-un lived. Its name means "House for Hunting the Ox." Hunting the Ox is an image for the Buddhist quest for enlightenment. Manhae was a Buddhist monk.

국밥

사람 사는 세상에 살면서
소머리 국밥을 먹는다
소들이 사는 세상에서는
소들이 사람머리 국밥을 먹는다

Rice Soup

Living in the world where men live,
I eat ox-head rice soup;
in the world where oxen live,
the oxen eat man-head rice soup.

타인

내가 나의 타인인 줄 몰랐다
우산을 쓰고 횡단보도를 건너며
공연히 나를 힐끔 노려보고 가는 당신이
지하철을 탈 때마다 내가 내리기도 전에 먼저 타는 당신이
산을 오를 때마다 나보다 먼저 올라가버리는 산길이
꽃을 보러 갈 때마다 피지도 않고 먼저 지는 꽃들이
전생에서부터 아이들을 낳고 한집에 살면서
단 한번도 행복한 순간이 없었다고 말하는 당신이
나의 타인인 줄 알았으나
내가 바로 당신의 타인인 줄 몰랐다
해가 지도록
내가 바로 나의 타인인 줄 몰랐다

The Other

I never realized that I was my other.
You, who scowl at me for no reason
as we pass on a crossing, umbrellas raised;
you, who always board first before I even get off the subway,
the mountain path that always gets ahead of me when I go
    mountain-climbing;
the flowers that always wither before they bloom when I go to see
    the blossoms;
you, with whom I had children, and lived in the same house from
    my past life on,
you have never once had a happy moment,
though I thought you were my other,
I never realized that I was your very other.
Till the sun finally set
I'd never realized that I was my own other.

뒷모습

그동안 나는
내 뒷모습이 아름다워지기를 바라는 사치를 부려왔다
내 뒷모습에 가끔 함박눈이 내리고
세한도의 소나무가 서 있고
그 소나무에 흰 눈꽃이 피기를 기다려왔으나
내 뒷모습에도 그믐달 같은 슬픈 얼굴이 있었다
오늘은 내 뒷모습에 달린 얼굴을 향해 개가 짖는다
아이들이 달려와 돌을 던진다
뒷모습의 그림자끼리 비틀비틀 걸어가는 어두운 골목
보행등의 흐린 불빛조차 꺼져버린다
내일은 내 남루한 뒷모습에 강물이 흘러라
내 뒷모습의 얼굴은 둥둥 강물에 떠내려가
배고픈 백로한테 쪼아먹혀라

Seen from the Back

Until now I
enjoyed the luxury of hoping my appearance from behind was
 growing beautiful.
Sometimes on my rear image, large flakes of snow would fall,
the pine trees from *Winter Scene** stood,
and I would wait for those pines to blossom white with snow,
but on my rear image was a sad face like a waning moon.
Today a dog is barking at the face hanging on my rear image.
Children come running, throwing stones.
In a dark alley where shadows of my rear image stagger along,
even the feeble streetlight goes out.
Tomorrow let a river flow on my shabby rear image.
Let the face of my rear image go bobbing off downstream
to feed a hungry heron.

---

* *The Winter Scene* (*Sehando*) is a famous ink painting from 1844 by Kim Jeong-hui, one of the most celebrated scholars of the late Joseon period.

백로

백로가 강가를 거니는 것은
부처님 말씀을 찾아나선 것이지
배가 고파 작은 물고기나 잡아먹으려고
거닐고 있는 것은 아니다

백로가 강 한가운데 한 발로 서서
해가 지도록 꼼짝도 하지 않는 것은
마음속에 부처님 말씀을 깊게 새기고 있는 것이지
헤엄쳐오는 어린 물고기들을
숨죽이며 기다리고 있는 것은 아니다

A White Heron

A heron strolling along the riverside is out in search of
　　Buddha's words;
it is not strolling about
just to feed on small fish because it's hungry.

The heron stands on one leg out in the river
not moving an inch until the sun goes down,
it seems to be pondering Buddha's words deep in its heart,
it is certainly not waiting breathlessly
for baby fish to come swimming by.

Part 5

벽돌

위로 쌓아올려지기보다 밑에 내려깔리기를 원한다
지상보다 먼 하늘을 향해 계속 쌓아올려져야 한다면
언제나 너의 발밑에 내려깔려
누구든 단단히 받쳐줄 수 있게 되길 바란다
어느날 너와 함께 하늘 높이 쌓아올려졌다 하더라도
지상을 가르는 장벽이 되길 바라지는 않는다
산성이나 산성의 망루가 되기는 더더욱 바라지 않는다
그저 우리 동네 공중목욕탕 굴뚝이나 되길 바란다
때로는 성당의 종탑이 되어 푸른 종소리를 들으며
단단해지기보다 부드러워지길 바란다
쌓아올린 것은 언젠가는 무너지는 것이므로
돌이 되기보다 흙이 되길 바란다

Bricks

Rather than being piled up high, they prefer to be laid out low
    underneath.
If they must continue to be piled high toward the sky
they'd rather be laid out underneath your feet
to offer anyone a firm footing.
Even if, one day, they are piled as high as the sky with you,
they do not want to be a wall separating the ground.
They do not, even more so, want to be a fortress or a fortress
    watchtower.
They simply long to be the chimney of our neighborhood bathhouse,
and from time to time they want to become a church tower
listen to the bright sound of a bell,
and become soft rather than hard.
Since all that is piled up must one day fall,
they would rather become clay than stones.

징검다리

물은 흐르는 대로 흐르고
얼음은 녹는 대로 녹는데
나는 사는 대로 살지 못하고
징검다리가 되어 엎드려 있다

오늘도 물은 차고 물살은 빠르다
그대 부디 물속에 빠지지 말고
나를 딛고 일어나 힘차게 건너가라
우리가 푸른 냇가의 징검다리를
이제 몇 번이나 더 건너갈 수 있겠느냐

때로는 징검다리도 물이 되어 흐른다
징검다리도 멀리 물이 되어 흘러가
보고 싶어도
다시는 보지 못할 때가 있다

Stepping Stones

Water flows as it should
ice freezes as it should
but I cannot live as I should
and lie flat, turned into stepping stones.

Today again the water is cold, the current fast.
Please, don't fall into the water
but stamp on me and cross over vigorously.
How many more times will we be able
to cross the blue stream's stepping stones?

Sometimes stepping stones turn into water and flow away.
Stepping stones turned into water flow far away
and there are times when they can never be seen again
no matter how much we want to see them.

용서의 의자

나의 지구에는
용서의 의자가 하나 놓여 있다
의자에 앉기만 하면 누구나
용서할 수 있고 용서받을 수 있는
절대고독의 의자 하나
쌩떽쥐뻬리의 어린 왕자가 해질녘
어느 작은 별에 앉아 있던 의자도 아니고
법정 스님이 오대산 오두막에 홀로 살면서
손수 만드신 못생긴 나무의자도 아닌
못이 툭 튀어나와 살짝 엉덩이를 들고 앉아야 하는
앉을 때마다 삐걱삐걱 눈물의 소리가 나는
작은 의자 하나
누군가가 만들어놓고
다른 별로 떠났다

Chair of Forgiveness

On my planet
there stands a single chair of forgiveness.
a single chair of absolute solitude,
and anyone who sits on that chair
can forgive and be forgiven,
not the chair that St. Exupéry's Little Prince
used to sit on at sunset on a tiny star,
and not the ugly wooden chair that the Ven. Beopjeong made
while he was living alone in a hut on Mount Odae,
but one small chair—
with a nail jutting out
so that you have to sit with your behind slightly raised
and every time you sit on it, it emits a creaking sound of weeping—
that somebody made
then left for another star.

사라지는 것들을 위하여

사라지는 것들을 위하여
나는 나의 가장 가난했던
미소 속으로 사라진다

어느 목마른 저녁거리에서
내가 늘 마시던 물은
내 눈물까지 데리고 땅속으로 사라지고
날마다 내 가슴속으로 눈부시게 날아오르던 새는
부러진 내 날개를 데리고 하늘 속으로 사라지고

이제는 쓸쓸한 저녁바닷가
수평선 너머로 사라지는 수평선과 함께
인간이 되고 싶었던 나의 모든 꿈조차
꿈속으로 사라져

캄캄한 서울
종로 피맛골 한 모퉁이
취객들의 밤의 발자국에 깊이 어린
별빛들만 사라지지 않고 홀연히
술에 취한다

For the Sake of Vanishing Things

For the sake of vanishing things
I am vanishing into my
poorest smile.

The water I always used to drink
on some thirsty street
took even my tears and vanished into the ground
and the bird that used to fly up into my breast, dazzling,
took my broken wings and vanished into the sky.

Now, together with the horizon vanishing
beyond the horizon on lonely evening shores
even all my dreams of becoming a human being
vanish into dreams;

On a corner of Pimatkol alley
in dark Seoul,
only the starlight remains,
deeply pooled in the night footprints of the drunkards;
it alone does not vanish
but suddenly grows drunk.

증명사진

주민등록증을
재발급받기 위해
넥타이를 매고 단정히
증명사진을 찍다가
눈물이 왈칵 쏟아졌다
슬픔 이외에는 아무것도
증명할 수 없어서
증명사진에 내 얼굴이
나오지 않았다

Identification Photo

To have my identity card
re-issued
I was having my photo taken,
tidily so,
wearing a tie,
when I burst into tears.
Because nothing could be identified
except for sorrow,
my face did not appear
in my identification photo.

물의 꽃

강물 위에 퍼붓는 소나기가
물의 꽃이라면
절벽으로 떨어지는 폭포가
물의 꽃잎이라면
엄마처럼 섬기슭을 쓰다듬는
하얀 파도의 물줄기가
물의 백합이라면
저 잔잔한 호수의 물결이
물의 장미라면
저 거리의 분수가 물의 벚꽃이라면
그래도 낙화할 때를 아는
모든 인간의 눈물이
물의 꽃이라면

Water's Flowers

If the rain pouring down on a river
were water's flowers,
if the waterfall falling over a cliff
were water's petals,
if the white foam of waves
stroking island shores like a mother
were water's lilies,
if the ripples on a peaceful lake
were water's roses,
if the fountain on that street were water's cherry-blossoms,
and, still, if the tears of all people, who know the time for flowers
    to fall,
were water's flowers

거미

이른 아침
백담사 가는 길을 걸을 때
나뭇가지와 나뭇가지 사이로 이어진 거미줄에
내가 평생 흘린 모든 눈물이 매달려 있었다
왕거미 한 마리
내 눈물을 갉아먹으려고 황급히 다가오다가
아침 햇살에 손을 모으고
고요히
기도하고 있었다

A Spider

Early one morning
as I was walking up the road to Baekdamsa Temple,
all the tears I have ever shed in life were hanging
on the spiders' webs strung from branch to branch.
One great spider,
who'd been approaching in a hurry, eager to gobble up my tears,
was now, hands joined
in the morning sunlight,
silently
saying grace.

새들을 위한 묘비명

여기
가장 높이 나는 새가 되고 싶었던
밥 먹는 시간보다
기도하는 시간이 더 길었던
새들의 노숙자 한 마리 잠들어 있다

Epitaph for Birds

Here sleeps
one homeless bird
that longed to be the highest flying bird
and therefore spent more time praying
than eating.

나의 방명록

나의 방명록에 기록된
인간의 이름은 다 바람에 날려갔다
기역자는 기역자대로 시옷자는 시옷자대로
바람에 다 날려가
실크로드를 헤매거나 사하라 사막의
모래언덕에 파묻혔다
어떤 애증의 이름은 파묻혀 미라가 되었으나
이젠 잊어라
이름이 무슨 사랑이더냐
눈물 없는 이름이 무슨 운명이더냐
겨울이 지나간 나의 방명록엔
새들이 나뭇잎을 물고 날아와 이름을 남긴다
남의 허물에서 나의 허물이 보일 때
나의 방명록엔
백목련 꽃잎들이 떨어져 눈부시다

My Guest Book

All the people's names inscribed in my guest book
have blown away in the wind.
The A's with the A's, the B's with the B's,
blown away in the wind,
have all gone wandering along the Silk Road or been buried
in a Sahara sand-dune.
Though some love-hate names have been buried and have turned
   into mummies,
forget them now.
A name is no love.
A name without tears is no destiny.
Once winter is past, birds come flying with leaves in their bills
and leave their names in my guest book.
When I see my own flaws in others' flaws
my guest book
dazzles with magnolia petals falling.

밤의 비닐하우스

밤기차를 타고
밤을 지날 때
환하게 불을 밝힌 비닐하우스는
밤의 갠지스 강을 건너는
작은 나룻배

물결 따라 어디론가 흘러가다가
잃은 길을
또 잃을 때
흔들리는 강물에 띄우는
꽃등잔불

A Night's Plastic Greenhouse

As I pass through the night
aboard a night train
the brightly lit plastic greenhouses
are little boats
crossing the Ganges by night.

When I go drifting on, following the current
and lose my way
then lose it again,
they are flower lamps
set afloat on rolling river waters.

이중섭의 방

제주도 서귀포
이중섭 가족 네 식구가
바닷게들과 가난하게 살았던
초가 문간방
솥단지 하나 달랑 입구에 놓여 있는
1.4평짜리 방 한 칸
그 좁은 방 안을 들여다보다가
깜짝 놀랐다
한라산이 방 안에 저 혼자 앉아
어깨에 쌓인 흰 눈을
털고 있었다

Lee Jung-seop's Room*

At Seoguipo in Jeju Island,
a thatched room by a house's gate
where the four members of artist Lee Jung-seop's family
lived with the crabs in poverty.
A room only 1.4 *pyeong*** in size,
with a solitary cauldron at the entrance.
Looking inside that tiny room,
I was astonished.
Mount Halla was sitting there all alone,
shaking off the white snow
piled on its shoulders.

---

* Lee Jung-seop (1916-1956) was a celebrated painter who lived in great poverty. He took refuge with his family in Jeju Island during the Korean War, and the room can still be visited.
** *Pyeong* is a traditional Korean unit of measurement, equivalent to roughly 36 sq. ft.

다산 주막

홀로 술을 들고 싶거든 다산 주막으로 가라
강진 다산 주막으로 가서 잔을 받아라
다산 선생께서 주막 마당을 쓸고 계시다가
대빗자루를 거두고 꼿꼿이 허리를 펴고 반겨주실 것이다
주모가 차려준 조촐한 주안상을 마주하고
다산 선생의 형형한 눈빛이 달빛이 될 때까지
이 시대의 진정한 취객이 될 수 있을 것이다
겨울 창밖으로 지나가는 딱딱한 구름과 술을 들더라도
눈물이 술이 되면 일어나 다산 주막으로 가라
술병을 들고 고층아파트 옥상에서 뛰어내리지 말고
무릎으로 걸어서라도 다산 주막으로 가라
강진 앞바다 갯벌 같은 가슴을 열고
다산 선생께서 걸어나와 잔을 내미실 것이다
참수당한 눈물의 술잔을 기울이실 것이다
무릎을 꿇고 막사발에 가득
다산 선생께 푸른 술을 올리는 동안
눈물은 기러기가 되어 날아갈 것이다

Dasan's Tavern

When you feel like drinking alone, go to Dasan's tavern.
Go to Dasan's tavern in Gangjin and accept a drink.
Master Dasan will put down his broom from sweeping the yard,
straighten his posture and welcome you.
Greeted with the simple food and drink prepared by the tavern lady,
you will be able to become this age's true drunkard
until Master Dasan's piercing gaze turns into moonlight.
Even if you were exchanging drinks with the stiff clouds passing
    outside a wintery window,
once your tears become liquor, rise and go to Dasan's tavern.
Don't jump off a high-rise apartment building carrying a bottle
    of liquor,
go to Dasan's tavern, even if you have to crawl on your knees.
Opening his arms wide as the mudflats off Gangjin,
Master Dasan will come walking out and offer you a cup.
He will drink the glass of beheaded tears.
While you offer Master Dasan
a bowlful of blue wine on your knees,
your tears will turn into wild geese and go flying away.

시집

어느 날
무심히 책상에 앉아 졸고 있다가
문득 시집이 꽂혀 있는 책꽂이를 바라보았다
임영조 시집『시인의 모자』
박정만 시집『잠자는 돌』
정채봉 시집『너를 생각하는 것이 나의 일생이었지』
김남주 시집『나의 칼 나의 피』
천상병 시집『귀천』
조태일 시집『자유가 시인더러』
신현정 시집『바보사막』
뜻밖에
앞서거니 뒤서거니 세상을 떠난 시인들의 시집이
마치 묘비명처럼
나란히 서로 추운 듯 몸을 바짝 기대고 꽂혀 있었다
생전에 내가 만나보았던
함께 차를 마시고 밥을 먹었던 시인들의 시집이
물끄러미
졸고 있는 나를 쳐다보고 있었다
나는 슬그머니 그 옆에다
『사랑하다가 죽어버려라』내 시집을 갖다 꽂고
다시 눈을 감았다

Poetry Books

One day
as I dozed sitting idly at my desk
I happened to glance at the bookcase holding poetry books:
Im Yeong-jo's *The Poet's Hat*
Park Jeong-man's *Sleeping Stone*
Jeong Chae-bong's *Thinking of You Was My Whole Life*
Kim Nam-ju's *My Sword My Blood*
Cheon Sang-Byeong's *Back to Heaven*
Jo Tae-il's *Freedom Says to a Poet*
Shin Hyeon-jeong *Foolish Desert*
unexpectedly so,
books by poets who left this world one before another,
   one after another
like so many epitaphs,
were lined up side by side, pressed together as if they were cold.
Books by poets I've met before,
with whom I used to drink tea, share meals,
were gazing at me
as I dozed.
Stealthily, I inserted my own volume
Love then Die among them
before shutting my eyes again.

눈길

희디흰 눈길 위로
누가 걸어간
발자국이 보인다
새의 발자국이다
다행이다

A Snowy Path

On the snowy path
can be seen signs
of footprints.
They're birds' footprints.
That's good.

젊은 느티나무에게 고백함

부석사 무량수전 배흘림기둥이
젊은 느티나무의 마음으로 만들어진 것을
알아도 너무 늦게 알았습니다
무량수전 무거운 기와지붕을
열여섯 개 배흘림기둥이 받치고 선 까닭이
천년 전
느티나무가 사랑했던 모란 때문임을
늦어도 너무 늦게 알았습니다
오늘 홀로 배흘림기둥에 기대서서
느티나무 무늬로 남은 모란꽃을 쓰다듬어봅니다
오늘부터 다시 천년 동안
무량수전 열일곱 번째 배흘림기둥이 되어
당신을 받치고 서 있겠습니다

Confessing to a Young Zelkova

I learned, but learned far too belatedly,
that the curved wooden pillars of Muryangsu Hall in
   Buseoksa Temple
were made from the hearts of young zelkova trees.
Belatedly, but far too belatedly, I learned
that the reason those sixteen pillars stood there
supporting the heavy tiled roof
was because of a peony that the zelkova loved
a thousand years ago.
Today, leaning alone against one curved pillar
I caress the peony that now remains in the zelkova's grain.
From today onward for another thousand years
I will become the seventeenth pillar of Muryangsu Hall
and stand supporting you.

점자시집을 읽는 밤

늙은 어머니의 잠든 얼굴 곁에서
더듬더듬 점자시집을 읽는 밤
두 주먹을 불끈 쥐고 분노하기보다는
눈물로 기도하는 사람이 되기 위하여
점자시집을 읽으며 잠 못 드는 밤
별들이 내려와 환하게 손가락으로 시집을 읽는다
시들이 손가락에 매달려 눈물을 흘린다
손가락에서 떨어지는 눈물이 시집을 적신다
그래, 그래
나는 이제 희망을 미워하지 않기로 한다
잔인한 희망의 미소도 더 이상 증오하지 않기로 한다
나를 사랑하는 방법이 오직 고통의 방법일지라도
견딜 수 없는 고통은 허락하지 말라고
희망에게 쓰는 편지도 이제 그만 쓰기로 한다
사랑은 날마다 나무에 물을 주는 것과 같은 것이라고
젊은 별빛들이 내 손가락 끝에서
환하게 점자시집을 읽는 밤

One Night Reading a Braille Poetry Book

One night as I feel my way through a braille poetry book
beside my aged mother's sleeping face,
one sleepless night as I read a braille poetry book,
aspiring to become someone praying with tears
rather than someone clenching fists in rage,
the stars descend and brightly read the poetry book with
    their fingers.
Dangling from their fingers, the poems shed tears.
The tears falling from their fingers wet the book.
All right, all right.
I resolve to stop hating Hope from now on.
I likewise resolve to stop detesting Hope's cruel smile.
Even if the only way to love myself is the way of pain
from now I resolve to stop writing the letter
imploring Hope to disallow the pain I cannot endure.
Saying that love is like watering a tree every day,
one night as young stars at my fingertips
brightly read a braille poetry book.

광화문에서

서울 광화문에
소를 몰고 가는 사람이 있다면
그 소가 경복궁 근정전 앞마당을
가래질한다면
나는 그 뒤를 신발 벗고 따라가
그 사람의 소가 될 것이다
하룻밤 사이에
송아지도 낳을 것이다
송아지의 잔등을 씻고 지나가는
봄비도 될 것이다
서울 광화문에 워낭소리 울리며
느릿느릿 황소 한 마리 몰고 가는
그런 사람 있다면

At Gwanghwamun Gate

If there is a man driving a cow
at Seoul's Gwanghwamun Gate
and if that cow plows the yard
in front of the throne hall in Gyeongbokgung Palace
I will take off my shoes, follow behind
and become that man's cow.
Overnight
I will give birth to a calf.
Then I will become a spring shower
that washes the calf's back as it passes,
if ever there is such a man
slowly driving along an ox
ringing the cowbell at Seoul's Gwanghwamun Gate.

폭설

폭설이 내린 날
칼 한 자루를 들고
화엄사 대웅전으로 들어가
나를 찾는다
어릴 때 내가 만든 눈사람처럼
부처님이 졸다가 빙긋이 웃으신다
나는 결국 칼을 내려놓고 운다
칼이 썩을 때까지
칼의 뿌리까지 썩을 때까지
썩은 칼의 뿌리에
흰 눈이 덮일 때까지
엎드려 운다

Snowstorm

One day during a snowstorm
I entered the main hall of Hwaeomsa Temple
holding a knife
in search of myself.
Like the snowman I made as a child
Buddha wakes from a doze and smiles.
In the end I put down the knife and weep.
Until the knife rots
until it rots to its very roots
until white snow rises to cover
the rotten knife's roots
I lie face down and weep.

부평역

봄비 내리는 부평역
마을버스 정류장 앞
허연 비닐을 뒤집어쓰고
다리 저는 아주머니
밤 깊도록 꽃을 판다
사람들마다 봄이 되라고
살아갈수록 꽃이 되라고
팔다 남은 노란 프리지어 한 묶음
젊은 역무원에게 슬며시
수줍은 듯 건네주고
승강장 노란 불빛 사이로
허옇게 쏟아지는 봄비 속을
절룩절룩 떠나간다
동인천행 막차를 타고
다운증후군 아들의
어린 손을 꼭 잡고

Bupyeong Station

Spring rain falls at Bupyeong station.
By the neighborhood bus stop
a limping woman
shrouded in white plastic,
sells flowers late into the night,
telling everyone to turn into spring,
to turn into flowers as life goes on.
Shyly handing over
to the young station clerk on duty
the last remaining bunch of yellow freesias,
the woman goes limping off
into the spring rain falling white
amid the yellow lights along the platform.
She boards the last train for East Incheon
firmly grasping the hand
of her son, who has Down syndrome.

목련

목줄을 쥐고
내가 개를 끌고 가지만
실은 개가 나를
끌고 가는 것이다
봄이 왔다고
목련을 보러 가자고
개가 나를 끌고
백목련 속으로
걸어들어가는 것이다

Magnolia

Though I am holding the leash
and pulling the dog along,
in reality it's the dog
that's pulling me along.
Telling me that spring has come,
that we should go see the magnolias,
the dog pulls me
and into the white magnolias
we walk.

성배

친구여
아직도 성배를 찾아
떠나고 있는가
우리가 인사동에서
막걸리를 마시던
그 잔을 기억하는가
그 막사발에 담아 마시던
피와 눈물을 기억하는가
지금까지
우리가 마신 잔은
다 성배였다

The Holy Grail

My friend,
are you still setting out
in quest of the Holy Grail?
Do you remember the cup
in which we used to drink *makgeolli*
in Insa-dong?
Do you remember the blood and tears
we used to drink from that bowl?
The cups we have drunk from
until now
were all holy grails.

늪

지금부터
절망의 늪에 빠졌다고 말하지 않겠다
남은 시간이
한 시간도 채 되지 않는다 할지라도
희망의 늪에 빠졌다고 말하겠다
절망에는 늪이 없다
늪에는 절망이 없다
만일 절망에 늪이 있다면
희망에도 늪이 있다
희망의 늪에는
사랑해야 할 사람들이 가득 빠져 있다

Swamp

From now on
I will never say that I have fallen into the Swamp of Despair.
Even if the time remaining
is less than an hour,
I will say that I have fallen into the Swamp of Hope.
There is no swamp in despair.
There is no despair in a swamp.
If there is a swamp in despair
then there is a swamp in hope too.
The Swamp of Hope
is full of people I must love

번역자의 말

정호승 같은 널리 사랑 받는 시인의 시를 번역한다는 것은 굉장한 도전입니다. 정호승 시인을 아끼는 수많은 한국 독자들은 첫 시집이 출간된 1979년부터 그의 시를 접해왔고, 시인의 낭송과 발언을 직접 들을 기회도 많았습니다. 욕망, 사랑, 아름다움, 시간, 고통, 상실, 죽음 등 삶의 중요한 주제를 섬세하게 다루는 그의 시 세계는 오랫동안 독자들의 각별한 사랑을 받아왔습니다. 그리고 시인이 예순여섯이 된 지금, 비로소 그의 시들이 처음으로 영어로 번역되었습니다. 이제 한국어를 알지 못하는 독자들도 그토록 많은 사랑을 받아온 정호승 시인의 탁월한 문학성을 발견하고, 기쁨과 슬픔이 불가분하게 얽혀 있는 인간 존재의 역설을 향한 그의 탐험에 기꺼이 동참할 수 있기를 바랍니다.

우리는 본래의 시어에 가능한 한 충실하게 번역하고자 했으며, 동시에 한국어와는 전혀 다른 언어에 담아낸 이 시들이 그 자체로 온전한 영어 문학으로 독자들에게 다가갈 수 있기를 기대합니다. 정호승의 시에는 인류 보편의 지혜가 담겨 있으며, 이 지혜는 믿음이 뿌리내리는 곳, 다시 말해 인간 존재의 형이상학적, 비가시적 차원을 인식하도록 독자들을 이끕니다. 때로는 난해하지만 마음을 울리며, 눈을 밝히고, 생각의 깊이를 더합니다. 이 시들이 많은 독자들의 마음 깊은 곳에 똑바로 다가가 사랑보다 중한 것은 없다는 메시지를 전하기를 바랍니다. 오로지 사랑만이 다함이 없습니다.

안선재 · 수잔 황

Translators' Note

It is something of a challenge to translate the poems of a poet as widely loved as Jeong Ho-seung. His many Korean admirers have been reading his poems since his first collection appeared in 1979 and they have also had many chances to hear him read and speak in person. His delicately nuanced treatment of such vital themes as desire, love, beauty, time, pain, loss, and death has long made him a special favorite among readers. Now, suddenly, when he is already sixty-six years old, large numbers of his poems are to be made available in English translation for the first time. It is our hope that many readers who know no Korean will now discover the special qualities which have made him so beloved and gladly follow his explorations of the paradoxes of human existence, where joys and sorrows are inextricably joined.

We have tried to be as faithful as possible to the words of the original poems but at the same time we hope that our versions will work as English poems, using the words provided by a language that is very different from Korean. The wisdom embodied in the collected poems of Jeong Ho-seung is universal in its scope, leading readers toward an awareness of the metaphysical, invisible dimensions of human existence, where faith is rooted. Challenging these poems may sometimes be, but above all they are moving, enlightening, and insightful. We hope that they will speak clearly to the hearts of many readers, telling them simply that nothing matters but love. It alone endures.

Brother Anthony and Susan Hwang

About the Translators 번역자 소개

Brother Anthony of Taizé (An Sonjae) was born in 1942 in the UK. He studied Medieval and Modern Languages at Oxford and in 1969 he joined the Taizé Community in France. He taught English literature at Sogang University, Seoul, for nearly three decades. Since 1990 he has published some forty volumes of translated works by such esteemed Korean authors as Ku Sang, Ko Un, Cheon Sang-byeong, Shin Kyeong-nim, Park Ynhui, Yi Mun-yol, and Do Jong-hwan. Since January 2011 he has been president of the Royal Asiatic Society's Korea branch. He received the Korean government's Award of Merit, Jade Crown class, in October 2008 for his work to spread knowledge of Korean literature throughout the world. In 2015 he was awarded an honorary MBE (Member of the British Empire) by Queen Elizabeth for his contributions to Anglo-Korean relations.

안선재는 1942년 영국에서 태어나 옥스퍼드 대학에서 중세, 근대 언어를 공부한 후 1969년에 프랑스 Taizé 공동체에 입학했다. 30년 가까이 한국 서강대학교에서 영문학을 가르쳤으며, 1990년부터 구상, 고은, 천상병, 신경림, 박이문, 이문열, 도종환 등 한국 저명 작가들의 작품 40여 편을 번역하였다. 2011년부터 왕립아시아학회 한국지부 회장으로 재직하고 있으며, 2008년 한국문학을 세계에 알린 노력을 인정 받아 한국 정부로부터 옥관문화훈장을 받았다. 2015년에는 한영 양국관계 발전에 기여한 공로로 엘리자베스 여왕으로부터 명예 MBE를 수여 받았다.

Susan Hwang is assistant professor of contemporary Korean literature and cultural studies at Indiana University in Bloomington. She recently completed her doctoral dissertation at the University of Michigan in Ann Arbor on the shifting relations between literature and dissident politics in South Korea from the 1960s to the present.

수잔 황은 인디애나 대학교에서 한국 현대문학 및 문화연구학과 조교수로 재직하고 있으며, 최근 미시간 대학교에서 1960년대부터 현재에 이르는 한국의 문학과 반체제 정치운동 간의 관계 변화를 주제로 한 박사논문을 마쳤다.

Credits

Author	Jeong Ho-seung
Translator	Brother Anthony of Taizé, Susan Hwang
Publisher	Kim Hyunggeun
Editor	Kim Eugene
Copy Editor	Felix Im
Designer	Jung Hyun-young